ELEMENTARY SCHOOL PHYSICAL EDUCATION READINGS

PAUL A. METZGER, Jr.
Wordsworth Academy,
Fort Washington, Pennsylvania

WM. C. BROWN COMPANY PUBLISHERS
Dubuque, Iowa

PHYSICAL EDUCATION

Consulting Editor

Aileene Lockhart
Texas Woman's University

HEALTH

Consulting Editor

Robert Kaplan
The Ohio State University

PARKS AND RECREATION

Consulting Editor

David Gray
California State University, Long Beach

ELEMENTARY SCHOOL PHYSICAL EDUCATION READINGS

This work is dedicated to the
children of the Audubon, New Jersey
School System who taught me so much.

Contents

V PHYSICAL EDUCATION FOR THE ATYPICAL CHILD

SECTION THREE—WHAT DID THEY LEARN?

VI THE VALUE OF TESTING

Preface

The interest in and acceptance of the place of physical education in the elementary school continues to increase. Educators and parents have come to the realization that postponing the inclusion of physical education in the school curriculum until junior high school is untenable.

In light of this, it is important that prospective teachers, both physical education majors and elementary majors, receive considerable training in the field of physical education. This book of readings was developed to implement this objective. It can be used either as a text in itself or as a supplementary source of information. Although directed at the college student, it will also prove valuable to the elementary teacher already involved in his career.

Section One, "Why Teach Physical Education?" is devoted to articles which discuss the importance of having physical education in the elementary school. The contributions which such a program makes to the students' physical, social, mental, and emotional development are covered.

"Some Teaching Suggestions" which constitutes the second section of the book, includes articles which emphasize the how of elementary school physical education. The articles in this section are arranged in two groups: those which pertain to the typical child and those directed toward atypical children. The reader will discover that much of the information directed toward one of these groups can be used in working with the other.

The third section, "What Did They Learn?" is directed to articles which deal with evaluative techniques which can be used to ascertain both the improvement in student status and the condition of the program itself.

Acknowledgements

1. "Play Is Education" by N. V. Scarfe. *Childhood Education,* November 1962 Vol. 39, No. 3. Reprinted by permission of N. V. Scarfe and the Association for Childhood Education International. Copyright (c) 1962 by the Association.
2. "Play Is Valid" by Lawrence K. Frank. *Childhood Education,* March 1968 Vol. 44, No. 7. Reprinted by permission of Lawrence K. Frank and the Association for Childhood Education International. Copyright (c) 1968 by the Association.
3. "The Role of Play in Child Development" by Lawrence K. Frank. *Childhood Education,* October 1964. Reprinted by permission of Lawrence K. Frank and the Association for Childhood Education International. Copyright (c) 1964 by the Association.
4. "Accomplishing Our Educational Purpose Through Game Activities" by Thomas J. Sheehan. *The Physical Educator,* March 1969.
5. "The Great Balancing Act: Eating vs. Activity" from *Your Weight and How to Control It* by Morris Fishbein. Reprinted by permission of Doubleday and Company, Inc. Copyright (c) 1963 by Nelson Doubleday, Inc.
6. "Inactivity Complicates Fat Child's Problem" from *Today's Health,* Published by the American Medical Association, December 1963.
7. "The Role of Exercise in Our Contemporary Society" by Kenneth H. Cooper. *Journal of Health, Physical Education, and Recreation,* May 1969.
8. "Does Physical Fitness Belong In the Schools?" by Charles Tobey. *The Physical Educator,* October 1969.
9. "Quality Physical Education—a School Responsibility" by Charles B. Wilkinson. In *Journal of the New York State School Boards Association, Inc.,* December 1967, *Education Digest,* March 1968.
10. "Recent Developments in Mind-Body Relationships" by Joseph J. Gruber and A. H. Ismail. Reprinted from the September-October 1968 issue of *Education.* Copyright 1968 by the Bobbs-Merrill Company, Inc.
11. "Health, Physical Education, and Academic Achievement" by Charles A. Bucher. *NEA Journal,* May 1965.
12. "Physical Education and Recreation as Adjuncts to the Education of the Mentally Retarded" by Julian U. Stein. *The Physical Educator,* May 1967.
13. "Learning About Movement" by Naomi Allenbaugh. *NEA Journal,* March 1967.
14. "Social Development—The Forgotten Objective?" by Joseph B. Oxendine. *Journal of Health, Physical Education, and Recreation,* May 1966.
15. "Making School Learned Physical Education A Continuing Force For Future Fitness" by Julian A. Stein. *The Physical Educator,* October 1963.
16. "An Emphasis On Elementary School Physical Education—Goal: A Superior Program For All" by John Puckett. *The Physical Educator,* May 1965.
17. "Elementary School Physical Education" by Margaret Miller. *The Physical Educator,* October 1968.

18. "Individualized Physical Activity" by Jean M. Young. *NEA Journal,* December 1965.
19. "Physical Education in the Elementary School" by Paul Smith. *Educational Leadership,* March 1963. Reprinted with permission of the Association for Supervision and Curriculum Development and Paul Smith, Copyright (c) March 1963 by the Association for Supervision and Curriculum Development.
20. "The Developmental Approach" by Thomas R. Burke. *The Physical Educator,* May 1970.
21. "A New Look at Elementary School Physical Education" by Francis Harms. *The Physical Educator,* October 1967.
22. "Creativity in Physical Education" by Billy Jean Little. *The Physical Educator,* May 1967.
23. "Seven Guides to Creativity" by E. Paul Torrance. *Journal of Health, Physical Education, and Recreation,* April 1965.
24. "The Movement Education Approach to Teaching in English Elementary Schools" by Shirley Howard. *Journal of Health, Physical Education, and Recreation,* January 1967.
25. "The Cargo Net" by John S. Hichwa. *Journal of Health, Physical Education, and Recreation,* January 1970.
26. "Cargo Net Capers" by John Kautz. From *Instructor,* Copyright August/September 1970, The Instructor Publications, Inc.
27. "Physical Education in the Nursery School Program" by Bernard Wolf. *Journal of Health, Physical Education, and Recreation,* May 1966.
28. "These Are Your Children" by Gladys Gardner Jenkins. *Journal of Health, Physical Education, and Recreation,* November-December 1966.
29. "Helping Youngsters Read Through Physical Education Experiences" by Anthony F. Pegnia. *The Physical Educator,* May 1968.
30. "Track Endurance Training for Elementary School Children" by R. L. Wickstrom. *The Physical Educator,* March 1968.
31. "Jumping Builds Coordination" by Doyice J. Cotton. From *Instructor,* Copyright August/September 1969, The Instructor Publications, Inc.
32. "Elementary Physical Education—The Miniature Olympics" by Harry Oxford. *The Physical Educator,* December 1967.
33. "Weight Training for Elementary School Boys?" by Wesley K. Ruff. *The Physical Educator,* May 1962.
34. "Teaching Motor Skills to the Mentally Retarded" by Paul Dunham, Jr. *Exceptional Children,* May 1969.
35. "Some Psychological Factors In Motivating Handicapped Students In Adapted Physical Education" by John R. Schoon. *The Physical Educator,* December 1962.
36. "Social Groupings Enhance Recreation Opportunities for Retarded Children" by Vern H. McGriff. *Journal of Health, Physical Education, and Recreation,* January 1970.
37. "Creativity in Teaching Physical Education to the Physically Handicapped Child" by Dagney Christensen. *Journal of Health, Physical Education, and Recreation,* March 1970.
38. "Physical Education: A Substitute for Hyperactivity and Violence" by Thomas Edson. *Journal of Health, Physical Education, and Recreation,* September 1969.
39. "A Diversified Physical Education Program" by Donald Bilyew. *The Pointer for Special Class Teachers and Parents of the Handicapped,* Published by New Readers Press.
40. "Evaluation in the Elementary Physical Education Program" by Stratton F. Caldwell. *The Physical Educator,* December 1965.
41. "A Gap in the Elementary School Testing Program" by T. M. Scott. *The Physical Educator,* October 1961.
42. "Physical Fitness Appraisal in the Primary Grades" by William F. Straub and A. Mae Timer. *The Physical Educator,* March 1969.
43. "Sizing Up Your School's Phys ed" Reprinted by permission from *Changing Times, The Kiplinger Magazine,* (January 1968 Issue), Copyright 1968 by The Kiplinger Washington Editors, Inc.

WHY TEACH PHYSICAL EDUCATION

Introduction To Section I

It is essential that teachers realize why they teach a particular subject. A lack of knowledge of the basic underlying principles of a field frequently leads to unmotivational teaching. This section directs itself to providing background information concerning the importance of physical education in the elementary school curriculum and physical education's relationship to general education.

Although divided into three rather distinct parts, it is hoped that this section will lead the reader to an understanding of the affinity which exists between the physical, social, emotional and intellectual aspects of physical education.

CHAPTER I
PLAY AND CHILD DEVELOPMENT

Play Is Education
N. V. SCARFE

The purpose of this presentation is to demonstrate that play is the most complete educational process of the mind—Nature's ingenious device for insuring that each individual achieves knowledge and wisdom.

Play may be described as a spontaneous, creative, desired research activity carried out for its own sake. Because it is entirely natural, it is not necessarily moral when judged by the cultural or social ethics of particular people at particular times.

Theories

Play is in no sense a simple thing; nor is it explained or interpreted with reference to one or two criteria only. Play, in fact, is a very complex thing, as complex as the human being himself. There have been many theories of play and many criticisms of those theories. The rehearsal theory of Karl Groos, derived from his study of animals, has much to commend it because it postulates play as the means of growth and development and puts great value on it. He noted that play varied according to the level on the scale of evolution at which the various animals stood. The higher animals seemed to have longer periods of infancy and, associated with that, longer periods of more extensive play. Karl Groos's theory is, however, inadequate for the human child, for rehearsal of the complex activity of adulthood is clearly impossible. Further, it does not explain play by adults. Nevertheless, the idea put forward by Karl Groos, that play is a growth mechanism, is still fundamental.

The recapitulation theory of G. Stanley Hall was also an attractive, partial explanation of play; but both child and adult play have an important creative as well as repetitive element.

The superfluous energy theory was the one least able to explain the function of play satisfactorily. While children obviously let off steam at play, the energy expended is simply an incidental concomitant of the pleasure and enthusiasm that play engenders.

The only satisfactory theory is that which views play as an educational research activity. But first it is necessary to discuss the confusions that exist in people's minds about play and work.

Play and Work

Play and work are not opposites. They often coincide but should be measured differently. Work is measured by quantity of physical exertion. Play is measured by quality of emotional involvement. Unfortunately, "work" in public parlance seems to have borrowed emotional connotations. Work apparently is serious and important activity that ought to be done. Play is thought of as a frivolous and worthless waste of time in which weak characters indulge. This is a gross misrepresentation of the fact, because we know that when an activity takes on the characteristics of desired play then normally more effort is expended and more work done. Work and play are not opposites, and the sooner it is understood that excellent education goes on only when considerable effort is expended in the spirit of serious play, the better it will be for our whole educational system.

Therapy

In the past too much emphasis has been put on the therapeutic value of play in helping to understand the fears, the anxieties and the disturbances of mentally ill children. This emphasis has led some people to suppose that play is necessary only for those who are mentally disturbed or maladjusted as a kind of curative or therapeutic medicine. They overlook the fact that children become ill largely because they have been deprived of the freedom and opportunity to play. Play is as necessary to the mental health of the child as food is to his physical well-being.

Education

The concern here is mainly with the positive values of play to the "normal" well child or, put in another way, with the great value of play in education and with the importance that a teacher should attach to using this built-in provision for individual self-education.

Play is the finest form of education because it is, as Lawrence Frank, formerly of the Caroline Zachry Institute of New York, says, "essentially personality development, whereby the individual organism becomes a human being willing to live in a social order and in a symbolic cultural world."* A child's play is his way of exploring and experimenting while he builds up relations with the world and with himself. In play he is learning to learn. He is also discovering how to come to terms with the world, to cope with life's tasks, to master skills. In particular he is learning how to gain confidence. In play a child is continually discovering himself anew, for it is not easy for a child to accept the patterned conduct of the social cultural living and in many cases he must escape into fantasy.

Play is a learning activity. It serves the function of a non-verbal mode of communication or a figurative language which satisfies a felt need of young children. Play is educative because while thus employed the child is self-directed, wholly involved and completely absorbed. A child can completely lose himself in play.

Play has, in fact, all the characteristics of a fine and complete educational process. It secures concentration for a great length of time. It develops initiative, imagination and intense interest. There is tremendous intellectual ferment, as well as complete emotional involvement. No other activity motivates repetition more thoroughly. No other activity improves the personality so markedly. No other activity calls so fully on the resources of effort and energy which lie latent in the human being. Play is the most complete of all the educational processes for it influences the intellect, the emotions and the body of the child. It is the only activity in which the whole educational process is fully consummated, when experience induces learning and learning produces wisdom and character.

Creativity

Since experimental research, creative activity and emotional maturity are the essential elements in the best forms of education, as they are in the highest forms of play and work, it seems important to spend a few minutes discussing education.

*American Journal of Orthopsychiatry, Vol. XXV (July 1955), No. 3, pp. 576-90.

While we are prepared to accept play in preschool education, we neglect at our peril to make sure that the spirit of play continues throughout all school and adult educational studies. To be effective and lasting, all ideas in the mind must somehow be expressed creatively in some concrete form. This is sometimes called recreation, but it is never exact imitation. All recreation has injected into it the personal creativeness of the doer or play.

An educated person is one whose intellectual efforts have carried over to character formation, attitude development and esthetic sensitivity—or, as Aristotle would have said, "to wisdom and virtue." The late Boyd Bode is quoted as saying that "it is agreed on all hands that education is more than just a matter of learning facts and skills. Public interest is poorly served if attitudes and appreciations do not receive at least equal consideration. The things that are learned must translate themselves into terms of emotion and conduct if they are to be significant." Only by using the spirit and characteristics of play can this be achieved. Unless learning affects the attitudes and emotions, it is not good or complete education. The great thing about play is that it totally involves the whole personality of the child; in particular, it modifies attitudes, character and emotions. It is the carry-over from intellectual activity to emotional involvement which is the true characteristic of a complete education and of play. It is only in creative and artistic activity that this important carry-over takes place. This is why the artistic and creative element of play and of education is so important.

Research

Play is much more than rehearsal or recapitulation or vigorous exuberance, although it may contain all three. Play is essentially a research activity—an adventure, an experiment, a transactional process. It is motivated by innate curiosity and inquiry. It is the expression of a child's urge to find out and discover for himself how to live, how to be. Play has the joy of discovery, the satisfaction of creativity.

If play is thought of as a research activity, then it becomes a most important activity for children and the spirit of play a most important stimulus to mental activity for adults.

Artistry

Sufficient has been said to prove that play is Nature's research activity, Nature's experimental mechanism for enabling a child to discover how to live and how to grow up. But the glory of play is that it is also artistic, spontaneous and often independent of external needs and stimuli. It is probably the spontaneity of play that has caused the general public to use the term "work" as its antithesis, because work in the popular mind is effort required or imposed from outside or an activity determined by someone else. Play is free, because the child's activities in play are still a little tentative and uncommitted, are still capable of exploration and revision, of renunciation and replacement. In play he can manipulate objects, events and even people with less restriction than is imposed on an adult. It is, nevertheless, equally possible for work to have all the qualities of play. Shaw's definition of an educational utopia was, "A place where work was play and play was life."

A child's fantasy is essentially inventive and fancy-free. It is a high-handed treatment of inconvenient facts. Nevertheless, a great deal of spiritual and intellectual vigor comes from make-believe. A child investigates the world of things around him by manipulation and direct experiment, whereas he investigates the world of society by a mental experiment called fantasy or make-believe drama.

Thinking

Piaget emphasizes the value of thought in play. He says that symbolic play is egocentric thought in its pure state. He adds that a child wishes to enjoy a private reality of his own. This reality is believed in spontaneously without effort, merely because it is the universe of the ego and the function of play is to protect this universe against forced accommodation to ordinary reality. All play is associated with intense thought activity and rapid intellectual growth.

The highest form of research is essentially play. Einstein is quoted as saying, "The desire to arrive finally at logically connected concepts is the emotional basis of a vague play with basic ideas. This combinatory or associative play seems to be the essential feature in productive thought."

Provides for Play

If play is Nature's means of individual education, how then should a teacher act? In practice, where is the line to be drawn between direct teaching and the child's discovery of the value of a moral order by free experimentation? How can we get discipline or morality into play activity?

Obviously, teaching methods in schools must aim deliberately at feeding the impulse to intellectual play, to experimentation and to the development of concrete modes of self-assertion. It can never be stressed too much that a child must find *his* way to maturity, at *his* own rate, with *his* individualized capacity and limitation. We must provide adequately for play and at the same time respect the dignity of the child so that we do not invade his integrity either by neglect or coercion. A teacher must not stunt or distort personality development or overdevelop it prematurely. How does a teacher encourage animal behavior to become social conduct?

The teacher's task is not that of directing play but of removing obstacles to constructive freedom. Put more positively, the teacher provides materials, space, opportunities and experiences, knowing the children's abilities and interests at different stages of growth. Teaching should exploit the spontaneity of the individual; the teacher should act by suggestion and example, not by precept and command.

The teacher, therefore, provides materials such as building blocks, modeling clay, paint, water, sand, paper; space; time; freedom and affection. He arranges conditions so that children naturally want to learn and want to play, or arranges conditions so that Nature can effect an education. The teacher tries his best not to interfere with the spontaneity, the search, the intellectual curiosity, the creativity or the freedom; instead he encourages dramatic self-expression and artistic growth in a moral atmosphere created by his own example and personality.

The spirit of play is vital to all humanity: the basis of most of the happiness of mankind; the means by which humanity advances creatively, scientifically, intellectually and socially. The spirit of play is vital not only to childhood but to all mankind. In understanding children's play, we understand the key to the processes which educate the whole child. Because we live in a highly civilized world, all play activities need the kindly, sympathetic, understanding teacher who will provide materials, suggestions, kindliness, freedom and space— who, by example, will set standards of behavior and discipline with which children can experiment creatively to their own advantage.

Play Is Valid
Lawrence K. Frank

Probably most of those who read these remarks are already convinced of the great importance of play in child development, not only in the early years but all through childhood and adolescence and in adult life as well. But how can we convince those who are indifferent or opposed to play and wish to focus the child's interest and activities on required learning and the development of academic competence? How can their understanding of child development be enlarged to recognize the child's urgent need for play? Can we show them that play is genuinely productive and necessary if the child is to master the often rigidly structured program set for children?

Examine Courses in Schools of Education

Do the schools of education which prepare teachers and administrators provide an initial orientation and understanding of play? Do the formal courses in child development neglect play because it has not been studied by current research methods and techniques to produce the kind of quantified findings on selected variables given in child development texts? If we are to hope for a reorientation and a recognition of the vital role of play, we should critically examine the courses and programs in our schools of education, recognizing the often unspoken disapproval of play, except perhaps of motor activities and competitive games on the playground.

Spontaneity in Response to Activities

While many young organisms engage in play, the human child finds in play the activities and the occasions for discovering himself, his strengths and his weaknesses, his skills and his interests, enabling him to learn to cope with situations and events appropriate to his size and strength. But, of special importance, through play the child exercises his spontaneity and his reactions and response to what he encounters and has selected for his activity.

Playing and the use of play material, alone or with others, evoke his energies, focus his attention and direct his efforts on what is appropriate and congenial and, in so doing, foster his development as a young organism seeking to cope with the actual world he finds around him.

Since play, not only by children but by adults, is a universal activity, it may seem unnecessary to assert that play is valid. But within recent years there has been a strong movement to restrict the play of children, young and older, to adult-imposed patterns in order to promote formal learning, especially preparation for school. We need, therefore, to be reminded of the validity, indeed the imperative necessity, of play in human development.

Some perspective may be gained by recognizing that the child arrives as a young mammalian organism, with all the wisdom of the body, as Walter Cannon termed it—the varied inherited capacities for functioning as an organism which he must continually exercise in order to live, grow, develop, mature and learn. Recent studies have shown that those babies who, shortly after birth, are given opportunities for sensory and muscular activities develop and learn more than those who are neglected or deprived.

Play: Most Fruitful Learning in Life

During the first five or six years of his life, the child is expected to learn to cope with the world, natural and human. He explores and

manipulates and thus cumulatively learns about *what* and *how* ...
and, also in these explorations, he discovers himself. He endlessly
rehearses, primarily by direct contact with the world, his gradually
enlarging awareness, his patterned perceptions and his growing
repertory of skills. He also learns the names and meanings of what
he encounters, not only by being told in words but by making those
words personally meaningful through his actual contacts and
manipulations.

With his sensory capacities, the child learns not only to look but
to see, not only to hear but to listen, not only to touch but to feel
and grasp what he handles. He tastes whatever he can get into his
mouth and he begins to smell what he encounters. No program of
teaching and adult instruction could adequately provide for his own
personal observations, activities and direct knowing. But he can and
will, if not handicapped, impaired or blocked, master these many
experiences through continual *play,* as we call this seemingly
nonpurposeful activity which is actually the most intensive and
fruitful learning in his whole life cycle.

Learning Through Trial and Error

The world confronting the child is, as William James called it,
a "great blooming confusion" which the child has to organize by
putting into it some orderliness and meaning, some way of making
situations and events understandable. The big adult world, the
macrocosm, is too large, too complicated and often threatening to the
child who cannot cope with it; and so he focuses upon the microcosmic
world of play, as Erik Erikson stated some years ago, a world that
he can encompass through toys and play materials. To these he
imputes his often childish beliefs and expectations and also his
feelings, but by repeated explorations he gradually relinquishes some
of his more fantastic beliefs.

When he tries to make the world conform to his childish beliefs
and expectations, he is repeatedly confronted with the actuality of
situations and events, the ever-present threats and sometimes painful
consequences. But he can do this restructuring of the world only if
he is permitted and encouraged to try, to persist until he learns what
can and cannot be done; and play provides a minimum of risks and
penalties for mistakes. Play, as we see in many animals, is a way
of learning by trial and error to cope with the actual world.

Discovering Himself

To live in the public world, the child must learn what is expected
and consonant with the beliefs and expectations of his family,
especially the symbol systems (primarily language) by which his

society names, defines and interprets whatever it is aware of and has learned to perceive. But before he can or should relinquish his own highly individualized interpretations of the world and accept the prescribed social patterns, he needs a prolonged period of fantasy and make-believe in order to exercise his imagination and his spontaneity. He builds up his "as if" world and establishes his life space as his version of what he is told and expected to say and do. In this way he discovers himself (not self-expression, since he must first develop a self before he can express it).

We should always remember that everyone exists in a public world and carries on his life activities but, as noted above, each person creates his own life space, as Kurt Lewin called it, his selected version of the world which both recognizes and ignores what others may emphasize and insist as necessary for adult living. By observing children at play, especially with miniature life toys, we often can see how they are building their life space by the way they select and reject, combine and separate, and manipulate play materials. They gradually learn the difference between *my* and *thine* and develop an image of the self as *me, my* and *mine,* the target of others' judgments and activities.

Basic Patterns for Living

Accordingly, it cannot be too strongly emphasized that play is of immense and crucial significance in development, when many of our unique human capacities are being evoked and put into practice, especially when many of the basic patterns for living as a human personality are being learned. How important these play experiences are has been shown by students of personality development and especially by those play therapists who are dealing with the stunted, warped and emotionally disturbed children, including the shut-in, nonresponsive, autistic children. Since these children cannot, or will not, speak they may be invited to use a variety of play materials wherein they disclose their private worlds and otherwise individualized "problems" by the way they manipulate play materials.

Through play—including not only play with playthings but spontaneous play and dramatizations as well—many children by themselves can resolve some of their perplexities and clarify their feelings. Soon after a child learns to speak, he stops making overt expressions of his thoughts and feelings as he realizes this is not often safe and may invite parental correction or punishment. Thus he develops his inner speech and begins to create his own private world; he assumes an identity as expressed by the *I* who is the speaker and actor and learns to perform various roles.

Free Play of the Mind Before Formal Expression

While play may be focused upon playthings and situations and people, it soon becomes concerned with ideas, concepts and assumptions by which the child carries on his many "thought experiments." So many of the most fruitful ideas in art and science have been developed by individuals who were free to consider new and unexplored possibilities which they later translated into more formal expression. They seem to have retained from childhood a capacity for creative thinking and imagination as testified by many of the most creative thinkers as having found their inspiration in what might be called idle fancy and nonlogical thinking—the free play of the mind.

But, unfortunately, while this capacity varies from child to child, it may be repressed and constricted in childhood by lack of experiences and encouragement to speak freely, to explore, to "make-believe," and to test out his own thinking by play experience.

Imaginative Play Through the Arts

Especially important in play is the opportunity for a wide range of artistic, esthetic experiences—telling stories, spontaneous dramatization and role-playing, drawing, painting and modeling, group singing and playing simple instruments by which the child can learn rhythm and the use of his voice. Dancing, the dance drama translating a story into bodily movements, and simple group dances with chanting also foster imaginative play and provide experiences which contribute to the child's development.

The great importance of the arts in childhood is that they provide and can, if not rigidly imposed by misguided adults, foster and evoke creative activities—not masterpieces but rather the production of what the individual believes and feels as his own, not a copy of models, following set patterns. Those who grow up to become artistic in various media are the children who were encouraged to explore and experiment, to discover themselves with opportunities for developing their individualized potentialities. But all children need the arts as essential to their development as personalities, to enlarge their awareness and to cultivate their sensibilities for human living.

Sources of Renewal and Re-creation

As the demands and constraints of social living grow and are imposed upon them, adolescents and adults may find sources for renewal and re-creation by nonrational experiences, as in play, often an elaboration of what they enjoyed in early life. Indeed the need for nonrational experiences, for living as an organism and functioning spontaneously, may become increasingly necessary if adults are to maintain mental health and find renewed strength for being rational when and as required. But unfortunately many adults have lost the capacity for play and seek passive entertainment and distractions which usually provide very temporary and inadequate relief from tensions and worries.

As the foregoing indicates, the schools often ignore and wholly neglect what the young child before academic schooling needs to develop as a personality, with some capacity for spontaneity and creative experiences. If the young child has had ample opportunities for play, he is likely to be better prepared for academic study and disciplined learning. If he has engaged in play without interference or interruption, he learns to perseverate, to engage in purposeful goal-seeking activities which he, as an individual, invests with his own meanings and values as he translates his personal capacities and often unsuspected potentialities into concerted and rewarding activities and relationships.

Interpersonal Relations

Perhaps the most difficult learning confronting the child is concerned with his interpersonal relations, with adults and especially with other children, younger and older. Games with definite rules and imaginary boundaries provide repeated occasions for learning to recognize and to respect others, their property and their persons, and to inhibit the impulses and feelings that are not socially permissible.

But all this requires adequate space, facilities and play materials. And, above all, it requires understanding, empathic adults and older adolescents who will, when necessary, provide the definition of situations and the necessary restrictions, explain and interpret the possibilities whereby the child is helped to learn to live with others. Especially in the formal school years, children need play to relax and to release tensions in various ways when they have been immobilized for some time and have had to submit to an imposed but often unwelcome regimen.

Pressure for Academic Achievement Fosters Frustration

As Otto Rank remarked some years ago in his book, *Modern Education,** every generation uses children for its own purposes. Today the pressure for academic achievement, cognitive learning and preparation for the next grade seems to be an expression of this contemporary desire to exploit children for what is often self-defeating purposes. This is interpreted as necessary to provide trained, skilled and knowledgeable recruits for business and industry,

*Otto Rank, *Modern Education* (New York: Alfred Knopf, 1932).

for science and technology, and for scholarship. As we are discovering, we may be highly successful in this program but foster unhappy and frustrated personalities who are neglectful or indifferent to human needs and feelings.

Many of our adolescents are expressing their discontent and even open revolt against the educational establishment which, according to many recent studies, exhibits a strong resistance to change. Many schools are unwilling or reluctant to give adequate time for play, for artistic activities and nonacademic interests. They refuse to recognize that most of the basic learning for living and social life cannot be taught formally but must be learned through daily living, playing and enjoying the opportunities at each stage of the life cycle.

Exploration Through Play

We should recognize that children from their earliest years are actively curious and exploratory and seek through play ways of coping with the world in their own individualized patterns. But unfortunately many are suppressed and robbed of their spontaneity and denied the opportunities they need for learning and growing. The integrity of the child as an organism-personality who through play comes to terms with the world and himself should be preserved. It is unfortunate that the term *play* has long been interpreted to mean idle and unproductive activity, for in truth it embraces a wide range of spontaneous and productive experiences.

SUGGESTED READINGS

ERIKSON, ERIK. *Childhood and Society.* New York: W. W. Norton & Co., Inc., 1950.
GHISELIN, BREWSTER. *Creative Process.* New York: New American Library, 1952.
HARTLEY, RUTH, FRANK, LAWRENCE AND GOLDENSON, ROBERT. *Understanding Children's Play.* New York: Columbia University Press, 1952.
HARTLEY, RUTH AND GOLDENSON, ROBERT. *The Complete Book of Children's Play.* New York: Crowell Press, 1957 and 1963.
MOUSTAKAS, CLARK E. AND BERSON, MINNIE. *The Young Child in School.* New York: Whiteside, Inc. and William Morrow & Co., 1956.
MURPHY, LOIS, ET AL. *Methods for the Study of Personality in Young Children.* New York: Basic Books, Inc., 1956.

The Role of Play in Child Development

LAWRENCE K. FRANK

Play provides occasions for children to exercise their varied capacities in spontaneous activities which are largely self-rewarding and usually enjoyable. Today the constraints of urban living and the limitations of space, time and freedom are depriving children of opportunities and facilities for play essential for their normal wholesome development.

The many programs for organized play and more or less regimented exercises and physical training now being offered or required seem to overlook or deliberately reject the importance, if not the necessity, of play for wholesome growth and development and for the maintenance of bodily functioning.

A child, we should remember, is initially a young organism with all the "wisdom of the body," as Walter Cannon called these inherited capacities for self-organization, self-regulation and self-repair. The child inherits not only specific patterns from his parents and grandparents but also functional capacities evolved by his mammalian and premammalian ancestors. These give him the amazing potentialities exhibited only by humans.

This mammalian evolution occurred over millions of years during which organisms were in continual contact and were learning to carry on their intercourse with the environment, an environment with a variety of ever-changing impacts and demands: heat and cold, barometric pressures, wetness and dryness, and the constant pull of gravity. Against these impacts man early learned to develop and maintain an upright stance and bipedal locomotion.

The human child is a product of long experience in living in a natural environment requiring great flexibility and adaptiveness and in coping with the often hazardous and threatening situations that demand alertness and quick reactions and frequently sustained exertion for survival.

Physiologically Deprived

Today we are discovering that absence of these environmental demands may bring a progressive loss or impairment of functional capacities, since the various bodily processes must be continually exercised if they are to be efficient and capable of sustaining the many operations essential to wholesome living. Automobiles and buses, elevators and moving stairways, air conditioning, and many hours spent indoors at sedentary occupations are beginning to impose a "physiological deprivation" that may be as serious as the sensory deprivations of which recently we have been made aware.

The young child (even in infancy if given opportunity) likes to be alert and responsive to the world, engaging in a variety of activities. Except when asleep, he continually explores, manipulates and relates himself to the world physically and through his senses. By grasping, hitting, pulling, pushing, creeping and crawling, standing erect and walking, and then running, the young child learns what no one can teach him, as neuromuscular articulation and musculoskeletal coordination, for coping with the environment. At the same time the child is engaged in what is not overtly exhibited or easily observed; namely, maintaining his organism by the continual replacement of cells, tissues, and the chemical constituents thereof, through these bodily activities that stimulate not only his incremental growth but this basic replacement growth.

Likewise, in his varied play activities, the child is fostering the progressive organization of his different organ systems and functional operations and learning how to maintain a dynamic stability that enables him to enlarge and reduce and to regulate all his bodily processes as responsive to his bodily movements and exertions. At the same time, these activities are developing his internal communications whereby the different bodily functions are synchronized and become more effectively responsive to the varying demands they must sustain.

The infant seems to act more or less randomly. But as he grows older and has opportunities for spontaneous, self-directed activities, he develops an increasing capacity for purposive, goal-seeking conduct. Unless obstructed and handicapped by others, especially in his play, he will show his own creative efforts to achieve what he individually projects ahead.

Play Essential to Health

If we deliberately ignore the psychological benefits of play, we can still say that play is essential to wholesome development of the young organism because in his play activities the child exercises these varied functioning processes essential to his health and well-being. But what is important is that the child does this spontaneously in his own individual way. He usually regulates the time, intensity and extent of his play activities by these inner regulatory processes that are difficult, if not impossible, for an observer to replace by external rules and regulations.

As children become increasingly subject to the constraints and demands of school, they are more or less seriously deprived of the kind of bodily activities described above. By way of compensation schools offer greater or lesser opportunities for periodical play activities or prescribe formal physical training and participation in games supervised by adults. More recently schools have been requiring children to engage in a program of "physical fitness" in which spontaneous play activities are largely replaced by drills and training in skilled performances, as in gymnastics.

Since the usual elementary school program in largely emphasizing academic learning and performance imposes upon children the requirement of sitting quietly and refraining from conversation while focusing upon symbolic learning, as in reading, children may be said to be deprived physiologically of normal and healthy development. Not infrequently there is an acute discontinuity in the life of the child as he is required to relinquish his immediate interests and enjoyment of the actual world in which as an organism he has learned to relate by a variety of bodily activities and manipulations, to accept the insistent demand for symbolic learning, as in reading and writing and mathematics, with the further requirement of physical inactivity that may often create a hunger for movement.

Recess and Gym Not Enough

It is assumed that a brief recess and a period of physical training or organized exercise will be sufficient to satisfy this hunger, especially since children will have an opportunity for play after school. A careful assessment of recess and gym periods may show that many children are building up tensions not adequately discharged by these intervals or afterschool play. Recess and gym periods are far from sufficient for large numbers of urban-dwelling children. The foregoing has given rise to serious questioning of the present conception of programs for physical fitness as not meeting the needs of the young child and the middle-aged child. Spontaneous play seems to be highly desirable—if not essential—to wholesome development and for relieving the stress and tensions of urban living and the increasing demands for intellectual achievement.

With the growing recognition of what has been called the "psychosomatic disorders and illnesses" and the realization that there is no functional separation of mind and body, there is a discrepancy between what we know is necessary for child development and what we are doing about it in our schools.

Advocates of a highly organized program for physical fitness apparently believe it possible, with only one or two hours a week of intensive training, to develop children's capacities for muscular exertion and endurance with little or no concern for what they may be doing the rest of the week in the classroom. A recognition of the "wholeness" of the child and of the importance of child development for our future national well-being calls for a critical examination of the assumptions and expectations of educators in all subject matter fields and academic programs. With the schools as primary agent for child nurture, education and conservation, the basic question is: What can and should they provide for the wholesome development of children at each stage in their sequential progress toward maturity? Known facts about children's needs and requirements, capacities and potentialities by various professions and disciplines studying children's growth, development and learning *can* and *should* be orchestrated into a coherent plan and program that will recognize and make operational two basic principles:

(1) that there is a regular, orderly sequential path from infancy to adult life along which each child will move if given opportunities and encouragement; for negotiating these transitions he requires the teaching which is appropriate for each stage in this sequential development, at his rate of progress, to attain his own size and shape and exhibit the capacities of which he individually is capable

(2) that each child is a highly individualized organism-personality with his own cognitive style and with aptitudes, capacities and potentialities rarely so distributed that he can achieve equally well in all the different subject matter areas or modes of physical achievement.

Especially important is the recognition of the child's unique organism and what can be provided during childhood and youth that will enable him to grow up and face the problems of later maturity and aging. Today's children are likely to live longer than any previous generation in the history of the world.

Play—Outlet for Tensions

A conception of play that recognizes the significance of autonomous, self-directed learning and active exploration and manipulation of the actual world gives a promising approach to the wholesome development of children, who need the opportunities and facilities that permit full functioning of their organisms if they are to meet the many demands, restrictions, pressures and tensions which they must encounter as they grow and develop. Children need help to become capable of bearing the burdens of freedom, for living in a free social order and contributing to the development of an urban, industrial civilization to which, as a nation, we are committed. This is one way we can show our capacity "to love little children" more intelligently and compassionately. It is a way to translate into the education of children our long-cherished, enduring goal values, a belief in the worth of the individual personality, and a genuine respect for the dignity and *integrity* of the child.

Accomplishing Our Educational Purpose Through Game Activities

Thomas J. Sheehan

We cannot escape the fact that education is the responsibility of the physical educator as he functions in our school systems.

Education not in the narrow sense of the word resulting in the acquisition of learnings in isolation, but education which demands the meaningful integration of behavioral learnings within the framework of society. The logical place for this kind of education is the game activity segment of physical education. It is imperative that at this time in history we have a renewed dedication of emphasis on the nature and function of the game activity as an educational medium.

Our Responsibility as Educators

We know education encompasses many forms and takes place in myriad situations. It may be assumed that the competencies and skills associated with physical education also will be gained in many ways. We find, however, that the actual teaching of physical education, in a formal, structured manner, reposes within the confines of the institution of the school. School physical education must be education for reasons other than the fact that it is offered in the school curriculum. It must contain within its offerings experiences which are directed toward the same end as that of the school. This end, according to the Educational Policies Commission, proposes that a student become conversant with the skills, knowledges, and standards of his society, and learns how it is possible to contribute to that society.

This purpose of the school imposes a considerable responsibility on physical education. When one learns the skills, knowledges, and standards of his society, his behavior is modified or strengthened. His behavior is modified relative to the standards of his society. This is an inescapable obligation of physical education if it is to be considered a function of formal education.

We who promote physical education as a phase of education may be inhibiting ourselves and our educational potential by neglecting the game activity segment of the total physical education experience. This game activity may range from those of low organization to the most complex forms; from tag games through basketball. It is within the game situation that we may find, upon further investigation, the real educational contribution of physical education—the kind of education which involves learning in a broad social setting.

Current Emphasis in Physical Education

To date, the lion's share of physical education research, conferences, professional discourses, and literature virtually have disregarded social educational learnings. These learnings have been sacrificed at the expense of the skill and physiological accomplishments which are but isolated parts of the physical education experience. Movement fundamentals, strength, flexibility, endurance, psychomotor learning, and exercise are but a few of the current focal points of attention. It is forgotten or misunderstood that these present focal points may be only means to a more profound and meaningful end, that is, the societal education of the consumer.

When we treat isolated learnings as ends we may be guilty of the hackneyed act of throwing the baby out with the bath water. What we do with movement skills is not specifically ours. What we do with strength, flexibility, and endurance does not belong uniquely to us. Music education, home economics, industrial education and visual arts education, among others, are all concerned with these learnings. What we do with the individual after he attains an indeterminate degree of proficiency with these competencies is specifically our domain. How we manipulate these learnings must be the consummation of our special contribution to society.

Home economics uses movement skills and physiological modifications in a special way. Industrial education uses these in a special manner. Physical education also uses these in a special way. We structure a game activity situation and call upon them for participation in that activity. When we act as teachers, in the context of a social institution, we cannot think of ourselves as exercise physiologists or movement fundamentalists. We must be certain that we provide opportunities for the modification of the individual as he behaves in society.

Functions of the Game Activity

What is the nature and function of the physical education game activity? At the present time this is obviously an academic question. The dearth of investigators relative to this phase of physical education dictates that only assumptions are in order. These can, however, be meaningful assumptions.

We provide opportunities through which the individual may become more competent in terms of his movement skills, physiological fitness, and perceptual-motor interpretations. If we treat these competencies as ends in themselves then the physical education game activity does not have functional meaning. Perhaps it would be more economical in terms of time to cancel our game activities. If physiological fitness is our special terminal function, then exercise programs are sufficient. We would be wasting precious time teaching game activities. If efficient and effective movement is our charge, then activities which would manifest only this aspect should be devised. Why be encumbered by the distracting idiosyncrasies of a game activity?

It may be stated, conversely, that the game activity is the culminating occasion for the interrelation of skills and acquisitions.

Here again there are nuances of the game activity which are foreign to these interrelationships. There are aspects of the game activity which bear no direct correlation with physiological fitness or movement skills. The specific knowledges associated with the game activity is a case in point.

Special Function of the Game Activity

It is precisely at this juncture that physical education game activities gain their special function as a medium for learnings which transcend the isolated factors of skill and organic efficiency. These isolated factors are integrated into a contextual experience which is at once larger than all of the isolated factors combined. Certainly, the interrelationship of isolated learnings is present but they become functional only as means of locomotion within the larger whole. The game activity imposes the additional elements of competition, cooperation, an environment containing peers, authority, subordinates, is task oriented, and has defined limits and boundaries.

As a result of these properties the focal point now becomes a social framework which only accidentally incorporates movement skills and organic capabilities. The learning which is possible in this situation is through the game activity using the tools of physical education (movement skills and physiological fitness) as intermediate processes. The learnings possible are the skills, knowledges and standards of the society. This is a portion of the kind of education with which we have been commissioned. This is education through the physical.

Conclusion

To accomplish our mission as educators our research, conferences, and professional discourses must take into consideration the educational implications of the game activity. If we adhere to the current practices and emphases in physical education, we may be compelled to dismiss game activities from our area of educational study. If we use them, let us use and develop them in view of their potential. This potential is the modification of human behavior within a social frame of reference—the game activity.

CHAPTER II
PHYSICAL FITNESS

The Great Balancing Act:
Eating vs. Activity

MORRIS FISHBEIN

Discussion of losing weight and sporadic attempts at weight loss occupy high priority in the lives of many Americans. This preoccupation with obesity has been stimulated by two forces: fashion and health. Neither fashion and fatness nor health and fatness are compatible.

Obesity is generally the result of excessive caloric intake in relation to caloric output—eating too much and exercising too little.

Obesity is a matter of balance—faulty balance of dietary intake and energy expenditure. Many people have a built-in balancing system that functions without conscious effort. As activity decreases, caloric intake decreases. Others must obtain this balance by consciously limiting intake of food and/or increasing activity.

Food habits and methods of food preparation go deep into the cultural patterns of races and people. Some primitive civilizations survived and prospered when patterns of eating habits were physiologically suited to their needs. Others disappeared from the face of the earth because of rejection or failure to establish adequate nutritional patterns for survival.

American food habits are based on the cultural patterns of many nationality groups. Some Americans retain more of the customs of their ancestors; others are enhancing their food habits by adding other customs to their own. Examples are the frequency of Chinese, Italian, Hungarian, Scandinavian, and American dishes being served in homes throughout this country.

The offering of food and drink has always been a symbol of hospitality. The gracious acceptance of the offering is another socially significant custom. Gatherings at the local drugstore, coffee shop, and club are as much, or perhaps more, for social contacts than to satisfy hunger.

Not only is social contact important, but also particular foods have special meanings. Sweets and desserts are used for reward and the withholding of these foods is a form of punishment. To our knowledge, hardly any child has been given an extra dish of carrots because he was good, nor has he had his carrots withdrawn because he was bad.

That man can overeat and gorge on occasion has been one of his weapons for survival. The Eskimo hunter has been reported to consume as many as 17,700 calories in a single day. The Eskimo also has periods of food scarcity. This need for eating excessively has vanished with the stabilizing of the food supplies. Food technology, improved transportation, home storage facilities, plus greater job security for most persons have eliminated the feast-or-famine type of existence in technically developed countries. There is still feasting, however, because of its social significance, and there is also some degree of fasting among certain religious groups.

Besides the social customs and availability of food, other factors may influence food intake of particular individuals. Many persons have observed that overeating may appease anxiety and may frequently be associated with feelings of insecurity. Persons who have been deprived of food early in life may resort to overeating in a situation in which they feel a loss of support. Similarly, parents who have experienced poverty in youth may almost force feed their children in their desire to give them everything.

Food intake balanced with energy expenditure determines body weight. Food habits, qualitative and quantitative, may be difficult to alter after they have been firmly established. Activity, unfortunately, is more prone to change, and lessens rather than increases with age. Food consumption may increase with age because of more earning power and more leisure. This is just the combination that leads first to overweight and then obesity.

According to life insurance statistics and common observation, men put on weight in the mid-20's and 30's while the increase in weight of women occurs later, in the mid-30's and 40's. This may reflect the activity changes of men, from active to passive participation in sports, and the laborsaving methods that have been introduced into industry. While laborsaving devices have lightened the housewife's burden, rearing of growing children still is a strenuous occupation and her increase in weight may come after the children are grown.

Insurance companies, on the basis of mortality studies, advocate that weights at 20 to 30 years of age should not be exceeded as one grows older. In accord with this principle, a new table based on data from the Build and Blood Pressure Study, 1959 (conducted by the Society of Actuaries) suggests desirable limits of weight for height for men and women of the United States. (See chart on page 22.)

DESIRABLE WEIGHTS FOR MEN AND WOMEN
According to Height and Frame Ages 25 and Over

HEIGHT (In Shoes)*	WEIGHT IN POUNDS (In Indoor Clothing)		
	Small Frame	Medium Frame	Large Frame
	MEN		
5' 2"	112-120	118-129	126-141
3"	115-123	121-133	129-144
4"	118-126	124-136	132-148
5"	121-129	127-139	135-152
6"	124-133	130-143	138-156
7"	128-137	134-147	142-161
8"	132-141	138-152	147-166
9"	136-145	142-156	151-170
10"	140-150	146-160	155-174
11"	144-154	150-165	159-179
6' 0"	148-158	154-170	164-184
1"	152-162	158-175	168-189
2"	156-167	162-180	173-194
3"	160-171	167-185	178-199
4"	164-175	172-190	182-204
	WOMEN		
4'10"	92- 98	96-107	104-119
11"	94-101	98-110	106-122
5' 0"	96-104	101-113	109-125
1"	99-107	104-116	112-128
2"	102-110	107-119	115-131
3"	105-113	110-122	118-134
4"	108-116	113-126	121-138
5"	111-119	116-130	125-142
6"	114-123	120-135	129-146
7"	118-127	124-139	133-150
8"	122-131	128-143	137-154
9"	126-135	132-147	141-158
10"	130-140	136-151	145-163
11"	134-144	140-155	149-168
6' 0"	138-148	144-159	153-173

*1-inch heels for men and 2-inch heels for women.

Note: Prepared by the Metropolitan Life Insurance Company. Derived primarily from data of the Build and Blood Pressure Study, 1959, Society of Actuaries.

Overweight has arbitrarily been defined as up to 20 percent above the median of the desirable weight range; obesity is a condition when the weight is 20 percent or more above this median.

In recent years, some investigators have used skin folds measured by calipers, rather than body weight, as a measure of fatness. The forearm and the area beneath the shoulder blade are usually measured. Another method, used in some research centers for determining body fatness and muscle mass, is by weighing under water. For practical purposes, however, a step on the scale and a look in the mirror is sufficient to determine fatness.

While ample evidence indicates that obesity seems to run in families, separating genetic and environmental factors is difficult. In animal studies, obesity on a genetic basis does exist. Children's food habits are based on the foods offered at home. Since obesity is most difficult to control when started in early childhood, providing an environment that will prevent obesity in children is important.

We have all heard our friends say, "I eat the same as he does and I am fat while he is thin." Let us take the case of five men. These men have the same stature and none need expend much physical energy in his occupation. The desirable weight for each is 154 pounds. The usual diet for each provides about 2400 calories. The food selection provides sufficient nutrients to meet recommended dietary allowances.

Mr. A. consumes only the usual 2400-calorie diet. He seldom eats between meals. Mr. B. eats the usual diet but likes bacon and an egg for breakfast. He also uses cream instead of milk, adds gravy to his meat, puts a "little" butter on his potatoes, and mayonnaise with his sandwich and salad. His meals, with the exception of breakfast, really look like Mr. A.'s, but these "little" additions add 1000 calories and that is enough to cause Mr. B. to gain weight.

Mr. C. eats just like Mr. A. The only difference is that he likes to relax with a few cocktails and canapes before dinner. He also likes a highball or two during the evening or a couple of glasses of beer. He is adding 1000 calories to his diet.

Mr. D. eats the 2400-calorie diet plus a couple of soft drinks, a cocktail or so, plus a snack at bedtime. He, too, is eating above 1000 calories more than Mr. A. Mr. D., however, still weighs 154 pounds. This is because he has stepped up his activity. He walks several miles a day, does setting-up exercises, and mows the lawn without benefit of a power mower. He even bicycles whenever possible.

These examples illustrate how a basic diet will vary with a few extras and how exercise will help counteract the extras. Mr. E. eats a menu that looks like Mr. A.'s. He uses less butter and mayonnaise, however, skim milk for whole milk, omits the brownie when he already has one dessert, the strawberries. Mr. E. is eliminating 600 calories per day and will soon lose the 10 pounds he gained during the year when he ate like Mr. B.

In 1930-1940, the emphasis for weight control was on modifying dietary habits alone. The beneficial effect of exercise was neglected. During the last decade, however, exercise has been found again to be an effective method of weight control, and, when used with dietary restrictions, is particularly satisfactory.

The chart below shows some of the approximate energy expenditures of some activities. To illustrate this point, a person might walk one hour at moderate speed, one-half hour at top speed, and dance one-half hour. These activities together will use up about 560 calories.

APPROXIMATE CALORIE EXPENDITURE
PER HOUR OF VARIOUS ACTIVITIES

Walking	
3 mph	270
4 mph	350
Cycling	
5 mph	250
10 mph	450
Horseback riding	150-600
Dancing	200-400
Gymnastics	200-500
Golf	300
Tennis	400-500
Rowing (peak effort)	1200
Swimming	
breast and back stroke	300-650
crawl	700-900
Squash	600-700
Climbing	700-900
Skiing	600-700
Skating (fast)	300-700

Thus, a person maintaining weight on 2400 calories would have a 560-calorie deficit if he engaged in these activities. If he ate 1840 calories instead of his 2400-calorie diet, he would be creating a similar deficiency. If he ate 1840 calories and did the extra exercising, he would have a 1220-calorie deficit, which roughly speaking would be about the same as being on a 1200-calorie diet without extra activity.

Another eating habit that results in overweight has been brought about by urbanization and industrialization: the hurried breakfast of coffee and a piece of toast, a light lunch, and then a large meal at night with little or no physical activity during the evening. Animal experimentation has also shown that serum cholesterol decreases when patients are fed six small meals a day, rather than one or two larger ones.

Some obese people are classified as "night eaters." These people eat very small amounts of food until five or six in the evening; then they consume large amounts of calories during the evening until bedtime. This pattern of eating, however, and compulsive eating generally, require some psychological assistance.

The eating habits of many housewives, particularly if there are children in the family, can be described using Mrs. L. M. as an example. Mrs. L. M. was a housewife of 40 who was 50 pounds over her ideal weight. She had three children aged six, eight, and ten. Mrs. L. M. had been reducing for years yet had never lost more than three or four pounds and had always gained it back a month after losing it. She only had two cups of coffee without cream or sugar and one piece of toast for breakfast, no lunch, or at most a sandwich and a glass of milk, and the evening meal without potato and usually without dessert. This came to approximately 2000 calories. But careful interviewing brought out these facts:

1. Mrs. L. M. usually ate one or two pieces of bacon when she was fixing breakfast for the family, or leftover bacon that the children did not eat.
2. The children occasionally left toast and jam on their plates, and she would eat it.
3. Frequently a neighborhood friend would drop by in the morning, and they would have some coffee (without cream or sugar) and a cookie or brownie.
4. In the afternoon tea or a cola drink were common.
5. Mrs. L. M. always kept chocolate or salted nuts in a dish on the living room table for the children to have or to offer friends who might drop in. She frequently helped herself when busy with her housework.
6. If the children did not finish all of their fried chicken or lamb chops when served at 5:30 she would eat the leftovers.
7. Before dinner at 7:00 with her husband, she would frequently join him for a cocktail.
8. Before retiring at night she always checked to make sure the kitchen door was locked, and since she usually had not had dessert at dinner, she frequently helped herself to a glass

of milk with some crackers and cheese, or joined her husband
for a glass of beer.

9.   Mrs. L. M. frequently made special cookies or cakes for her
children, and while she seldom ate them (except when a
friend stopped by for coffee or tea), she always sampled them
after they were made or had one or two before going to bed.

These habits more than equaled the 2000 calories received from
her poorly formed meals. An adequate breakfast, lunch, and dinner
with lots of fruits and vegetables solved her problem and within eight
months she reached her desirable weight.

Theoretically, the obese person can reduce his weight if he can
reduce his calorie consumption and/or increases activity. However,
his ability to adhere to a change in his food intake will depend greatly
on the understanding by both himself and his medical advisor of what
food means to each particular individual and the development of
insight into each situation.

Some individuals can reduce successfully with little or no
assistance from the physician or medical team, and others may need
extensive help.

We have found that persons with a good general meal pattern
(three balanced meals a day and perhaps one or two small snacks),
have less difficulty remaining on a reducing diet than persons with
unusual distribution of meals (such as omitting breakfast or lunch
except for a beverage) or those who eat large amounts of one specific
food.

Considerably more emphasis should be placed on the value of
regular exercise in promoting physical well-being and weight control.
More research should be devoted to finding out why people eat as
they do, particularly, care should be given in helping children and
adolescents develop and maintain good food habits. Prevention of
obesity is more effective than treatment after the obesity has
occurred.

A balanced diet means getting nutrients in amounts sufficient
to maintain good health and desirable weight. Good nutrition can be
achieved through a variety of patterns. The patterns will vary from
country to country and from person to person. There is not any one
best method of eating. Good nutrition means good habits of eating
—consuming meat, fish, poultry, dairy products, enriched and
whole-grain cereals and bread, fruits and vegetables—fresh, canned,
and frozen.

Good food habits are achieved by intelligent planning of meals,
using a variety of foods, and proper cooking. Good nutrition comes
from buying food at your grocer, butcher, and supermarket. The food

faddist will have one believe otherwise. The public should be aware of the misinformation and often harmful suggestions that the food faddist makes. Misinformation is especially prevalent in the area of so-called "reducing diets."

Considerable progress has been made in the United States in dealing with nutritional deficiencies. From data pertaining to food consumption in this country in the last 40 years, we know that the use of protective foods such as milk, cheese, citrus fruits, and tomatoes has increased. Vitamin intake has been further increased by the fortification of milk with vitamin D, margarines with vitamin A, and by the enrichment of white flour and refined cereals with thiamine, riboflavin, and niacin.

An increasing proportion of the population has distinctly better diets, although nutritional inadequacies are not yet completely dealt with, particularly when one considers the special nutritional problems of pregnancy, lactation, adolescence, and old age.

The most important nutritional problem confronting those interested in the health of this nation is the prevention and reduction of obesity. An understanding of the meaning and importance of food habits and the implication of that meaning for prevention and therapy will help to solve this problem.

Inactivity Complicates
Fat Child's Problem

6

Not even a calorie-controlled diet in combination with a planned recreation program will help an overweight child lose weight unless the child is induced to participate actively in the planned activities.

This was the conclusion of Harvard University nutritionists who used a movie camera to compare the activity levels of overweight and normal weight children as they participated in tennis, volleyball, and swimming.

The study, said Jean Mayer, Ph.D., D.Sc., associate professor of nutrition at the Harvard School of Public Health, has demonstrated that obese children are much less active than non-obese children.

The camera was set to take motion pictures for durations of three to five seconds at four-minute intervals. Some 28,000 separate short filmstrips were examined.

The films showed that during tennis, the non-obese child was inactive an average of 20 percent of the time, while the obese child was inactive 55 percent of the time. "The active player went after the ball," said Doctor Mayer, "while his inactive competitor attempted a return only when the ball was returned to his immediate vicinity."

In volleyball, a team sport, there was even less activity on the part of the obese child. The overweight player remained inactive about 82 percent of the time, as compared with 54 percent for the average weight competitor. Again the obese player tended to wait until the ball came within range before going into action.

During swimming, the overweight children were totally motionless 72 percent of the time. "They just stood in the water talking," said Doctor Mayer. The non-obese swimmers, by contrast, were inactive less than one-quarter of the time.

7 The Role of Exercise in Our Contemporary Society

KENNETH H. COOPER

Physical inactivity has become a problem in modern society, and when obesity, high fat diets, cigarette smoking, and stress are added, the end product is an alarming increase in incidence of diseases of the heart and lungs. Admittedly, such diseases are multifactorial in cause but inactivity appears to assume an increasingly important role. Exercise, in relation to preventive and rehabilitative medicine, is a new and rapidly changing field of research. However, medical scientists, not satisfied with the current state of knowledge about physical conditioning and training programs, constantly seek more information. Therefore, educators in health and physical education are expected to apply modern scientific techniques and provide the much needed data.

Contemporary specialists in health and physical education are finding their expertise in demand where it never has been previously. For example, several large industries now employ qualified health educators to implement physical conditioning programs directed toward reducing the absenteeism and increasing the productivity of their working force. Physicians seek qualified assistants in the management of patients entered in cardiac rehabilitation programs. Even the average "jogging" adult continually asks questions about his "preventive medicine program." In all of these programs, physical fitness is the common denominator, and the specialist in health and physical education must bear the responsibility for advancing the state of the art and answering many questions.

What Is Physical Fitness?

A question frequently asked is "What is physical fitness?" This expression produces controversy immediately, for no generally accepted definition exists. To a physician, physical fitness may imply merely absence of disease. To a weight lifter, physical fitness may be synonymous with large, bulging muscles. To a health or physical educator, physical fitness may be equated with ability to perform a specific number of calisthenics or to run 600 yards within a certain time limit.

In this paper physical fitness means only *cardiovascular-pulmonary* fitness, that is, a good heart, good blood vessels, and good lungs. This type of fitness is the most important, for a person's life depends upon these organs. Freedom from disease, or having large, bulging muscles is not enough. Without adequate reserves in the cardiovascular-pulmonary systems, a person is not prepared to meet the common or unusual stresses of daily living, that is, he is not physically fit. But how can you know when and if you have reached this somewhat mystical state of health? Let me attempt to answer that rather provocative question.

Changes in the Body Produced by Exercise

The efficiency of the heart as a pump improves in response to regular, properly administered exercise. The heart not only becomes stronger and a little larger, but also increases its ability to deliver more blood with each stroke, either at rest or during exercise.[1] One of the apparent results is a reduction in the resting heart rate—a phenomenon that can be documented by monitoring the resting heart rate before and after a vigorous physical conditioning program. Resting heart rates as low as 40 beats per minute are not uncommon in conditioned endurance athletes. Consequently the resting heart rate may serve as an indicator although not an absolute index of cardiopulmonary fitness.

A beneficial effect of regular sustained exercise is an improvement in the vascular system through which blood is delivered to the body tissues.[2] Of paramount importance is an improvement in the collateral blood supply to the heart, for it lessens the likelihood of succumbing to an occlusive heart attack.[3] This improved circulation provides some security for the normal patient and may help the cardiac patient who is actively involved in a rehabilitation program.[4]

The ability to ventilate large amounts of air rapidly is improved by regular exercise. Normally, obstructive pulmonary disease and weakened respiratory muscles interfere with sustained, high-level breathing requirements and limit endurance performance. Exercise-induced changes in the lungs and respiratory muscles, which modify this debilitating pattern, constitute another aspect of rehabilitative medicine.[5]

One of the most exciting changes observed in response to an exercise program is the change that occurs in an individual's personality. Exercising subjects tend to become less depressed, less hypochondriacal, and to improve their self-image.[6] They improve their self-image because they look better. They may lose weight, but even more commonly they lose inches. Inches tend to disappear at the waist, hips, and thighs and the weight loss may be in pounds if a dietary restrictive program is added. They tend to become less hypochondriacal because they feel better. In reality, they probably feel better because they are not sick as much. The reason a person becomes less depressed cannot be established at this time but the change is observed frequently.

Is regular exercise related to academic performance? This is another provocative question that cannot be answered readily. Some investigators believe that exercise helps to improve grades by somewhat subtle means. Actually, a student becomes more receptive and alert instead of more intelligent, and this may cause his grades to improve.

In one of the 12-week United States Air Force officer training courses, academic proficiency was measured by test scores and endurance capacity by performance on a 12-minute walk-run test. The relationship was startling, for in these 28-year-old men academic performance was directly related to endurance performance (see Table 1).

TABLE 1. 12-MINUTE PERFORMANCE AND
ACADEMIC RATING*

ACADEMIC RATING	NUMBER OF SUBJECTS	12-MINUTE DISTANCE (MILES)
Low satisfactory	39	1.41
Satisfactory	148	1.45
High Satisfactory	219	1.50
Excellent	135	1.51
Near Outstanding	33	1.54
Outstanding	35	1.58

*Sanders, James B. Jr. "A Solution to the Air Force Physical Fitness Problem." Unpublished Command & Staff College Thesis, Air University, Maxwell Air Force Base, Alabama, 1967.

Physical Fitness Testing

Physical fitness is quantified most accurately in a well-equipped laboratory, but this requirement is impractical for the rapid

evaluation of a large number of people. Therefore, it was necessary
to develop a field test of fitness that would correlate well with
laboratory measurements. Research conducted over a period of
several years indicated that a 12-minute performance test gave the
best correlation.[7] The subjects were given a medical evaluation and
then asked to cover the longest distance that they could *comfortably*
in 12 minutes. On the basis of this distance, each subject was assigned
to one of five physical fitness categories (Table 2).

Few studies have been made on students less than 17 years of
age. However, studies of 149 schoolboys from Luther Burbank Junior
High School in Burbank, California revealed that 62 percent could
exceed 1.5 miles in 12 minutes.[8] This finding makes a 12-minute
requirement of 1.5 miles not appear unrealistic for normal boys in
junior and senior high school. A 13:30-minute requirement of 1.5 miles
appears to be realistic for girls of comparable ages. Data for
establishing minimum requirements for grade school children are not
available. However, there is sufficient data to show that the commonly
used 600-yard and one-mile runs correlate poorly with cardiovascular-
pulmonary fitness.[9, 10]

TABLE 2.   12-MINUTE PERFORMANCE (MILES)

PHYSICAL FITNESS CATEGORY	AGE			
	17 - 29	30 - 39	40 - 49	50 - 59
Excellent	>1.75	≯1.70	>1.65	>1.60
Good	1.50 - 1.74	1.45 - 1.69	1.40 - 1.64	1.35 - 1.59
Fair	1.25 - 1.49	1.20 - 1.44	1.15 - 1.39	1.10 - 1.34
Poor	1.0 - 1.24	1.0 - 1.19	0.95 - 1.14	0.90 - 1.09
Very Poor	< 1.0	< 1.0	< 0.95	< 0.90

How to Develop a Fitness Program

The only type of exercise that will improve the cardiovascular-
pulmonary systems consistently is known as "aerobic exercise." This
designation applies to exercises that demand large amounts of oxygen
and distance running; cycling, walking, and swimming are excellent
examples. In order to meet the demands of these exercises, the body
must be conditioned to respond to an increased need for oxygen. When
this level of fitness is attained, the cardiopulmonary system improves
and the oxygen transport system becomes more efficient. Fortunately,
several methods can be used, for example, walking or cycling for long

distances at slow speeds, or short distance running or cycling at faster speeds.

The program of exercise can be adapted to people of all ages by using a point system. Exercise at a high energy level will be more effective in a specified length of time than low energy expenditure for the same period. The points assigned are multiples of the energy expended. Therefore, if the distance remains constant, the point value will increase with the speed (Table 3). Points may be awarded also for other activities if they can be classified as aerobic exercise (Table 4).

By using this point system, a progressive exercise program consisting of only one exercise or of a variety of exercises can be

TABLE 3. POINT VALUE FOR WALKING AND
RUNNING ONE MILE

TIME (MINUTES)	POINTS
20:00 - 14:30	1
14:29 - 12:00	2
11:59 - 10:00	3
9:59 - 8:00	4
7:59 - 6:30	5
Under 6:30	6

TABLE 4. ADDITIONAL EXERCISES*

ACTIVITY	TIME OR DURATION (MINUTES)	POINTS
Handball, Basketball, Squash	10:00	1½
	20:00	3
	30:00	4½
Stationary Running (80-90 steps/min.)	2:30	1
	5:00	2
	7:30	3
Swimming 25 yards (overhand crawl)	8:00	1
	6:00	2
	4:00	3
Cycling 2 miles	10:00	1
	7:00	2
	5:45	3

*Extracted from *Aerobics* by Kenneth H. Cooper, M.D. M. Evans and Co., 216 E. 49th Street, New York, N.Y., April 1968.

started. However, certain medical prerequisites must be observed before starting this or any other exercise program. For subjects less than 30 years of age a general physical examination within the preceding year is necessary unless there is a known medical problem, or a competitive athletic program is to be started. In such cases, an examination must be performed within the preceding three months. For those between 30 and 40 years of age a complete physical examination within the preceding three months is essential, including a resting 12-lead electrocardiogram. Subjects 41 years of age or older need a complete physical examination within the preceding three months, including a 12-lead electrocardiogram and an exercise electrocardiogram.

If the results of the medical examination are negative, the easiest method of entering an exercise program is to select an exercise of the subject's choice and start accumulating points. Over a 16-week period, the subject should work up to an average of at least 30 points per week (Table 5). Once the subject averages 30 points per week, he can feel assured that changes are occurring in his body.

TABLE 5. A 16-WEEK CONDITIONING PROGRAM

WEEKS	POINTS/WEEK
1-3	10
4-6	15
7-9	20
10-12	24
13,14	27
15,16	30

Factors Affecting Fitness

With increasing age, some decrement in endurance performance takes place. How much constitutes a physiological response to aging and how much an adaptive process is not known currently. In primitive societies, this age decrement in performance is less than in our modern society, thereby indicating the possibility of a considerable adaptation. The performance of 60- and 70-year-old athletes also tends to discount the idea that severe curtailment always accompanies aging.[11] However, a slower response to training is associated with age. As a person becomes older, it takes longer to "get into shape." Therefore, it may be necessary to allow 32 weeks for the 16-week training program if difficulties are encountered in reaching specific point goals.

Participation in athletic endeavors during adolescent years affects both endurance performance and response to training in adulthood. Many adults have no specific athletic skills, and some have benefited even from special classes teaching the art of running. If physical educators effectively teach their students the skills basic to various types of physical activity, as adults they will have a good foundation on which to impose a physical conditioning program. Adequate elementary and secondary school training is of particular benefit to military personnel required to meet and maintain minimum physical fitness standards.

Obesity limits endurance performance without respect to age. There is no consistent correlation between height and endurance performance, but there is an inverse relationship with weight. At the beginning of a physical conditioning program, this relationship is more significant than at the end, most likely indicating an improvement in the muscle/fat ratio.[12]

Cigarette smoking has been found to have a consistent effect on endurance performance. Among 419 airmen of the United States Air Force in basic training and entered into a special study, cigarette smoking had a detrimental effect on endurance performance.[12] When the airmen were placed in five groups based on their cigarette smoking history, those who never had smoked consistently exceeded the performance of smokers on a 12-minute endurance run (Table 6).

From this study, it was apparent that smoking as few as 10 cigarettes a day affects endurance performance significantly. If a student or exercising adult desires to reach his *maximum* endurance

TABLE 6. CIGARETTE SMOKING AND PERFORMANCE*
(419 AIRMEN BASICS – AVERAGE AGE 19.1 YEARS)

| | | Performance on the 12-min. test (Miles) | |
| | | BEGINNING OF | END OF |
SMOKING HISTORY	NUMBER	TRAINING	TRAINING
Never	128	1.47	1.61
Quit	64	1.44	1.57
Less than 10 per day	86	1.42[a]	1.54[b]
10 – 30 per day	131	1.43[a]	1.52[b]
Over 30 per day	10	1.35[a]	1.44[b]

* (JAMA VOL. 203, No. 3, Jan. 15, 1968; pp. 189.)
[a] .01<P<0.5 when compared with the never category.
[b] P<.001.

performance, he cannot smoke even 10 cigarettes a day. This observation should be taken into consideration when a young student or an adult becomes involved in a physical conditioning program.

Regular exercise may play an important role in the prevention and rehabilitation of many chronic diseases. These diseases include adult onset diabetes,[13] high blood pressure,[14] coronary heart disease,[3, 4] and pulmonary emphysema.[5] Many startling and exciting studies have indicated a cause-and-effect relationship, but considerably more research is needed.

Physical educators can make major contributions to these studies, but only if they base their conclusions on scientific facts and not on historical theory. They should not forget that "It is difficult to teach unless you practice what you preach." The challenge to the overweight, inactive teacher becomes abruptly realistic when, after he discusses the virtues of a physically active life, a student asks: "What do you do?"

The future of America depends upon the strength as well as the intellectual capacity of its youth. Building strong bodies in people of all ages will help to assure the strength and integrity of our nation, and on educators throughout this nation will fall the burden of responsibility.

Footnotes

1. Saltin, B., Blomqvist, G., Mitchell, J. H., Johnson, R. L., Wildenthal, K., and Chapman, C. B. Response to Exercise After Bed Rest and After Training. Supplement VII to *Circulation*. Vols. XXXVII and XXXVIII, Nov. 1968.
2. Petren, T., Sjostrand, T., and Sylven, B. The Influence of Conditioning Training of the Capillaries in the Heart and Skeletal Muscles. *Arbeitsphysiol.* 9, 1936, pp. 376-86.
3. Frank, C. W., Weinblatt, E., Shapiro, S., and Sager, R. V. Physical Inactivity as a Lethal Factor in Myocardial Infarction Among Men. *Circulation.* Vol. XXXIV, Dec. 1966, pp. 1022-33.
4. Eckstein, R. W. Effect of Exercise and Coronary Artery Narrowing on Coronary Collateral Circulation. *Circulation Research.* Vol. V, May 1957, pp. 230-35.
5. Christies, David. Physical Training in Chronic Obstructive Lung Disease. *Brit. Med. J.* 1968, 2, pp. 150-51.
6. Hellerstein, H. K., Hornsten, T. R., Goldbarg, A. N., Burlando, A. G., Friedman, E. H., Hirsch, E. Z., and Marik, S. The Influence of Active Conditioning Upon Coronary Atherosclerosis. The Hahnemann Symposium entitled Atherosclerotic Vascular Disease. Edited by Albert N. Brest & J. H. Moyer. Appleton-Century-Crofts, N.Y., 1967, pp. 115-29.
7. Cooper, K. H. Correlation Between Field and Treadmill Testing as a Means of Assessing Maximal Oxygen Intake. *JAMA.* Vol. 203, No. 3, Jan. 15, 1968, pp. 201-03.
8. Bigbee, R. A., and Doolittle, T. L. Luther Burbank Junior High School, Burbank, California, Personal Communication, Feb. 15, 1967.
9. Doolittle, T. L., and Bigbee, R. A. *Res. Quart.* 39:3, Oct. 1968, pp. 491-95.
10. Allen, C. L., and Bryan, A. C. Aerobic Work Capacity of 90 Military Cadets. Presented at the 39th Annual Scientific Meeting of the Aerospace Medical Assoc. Bal Harbour, Fla., May 9, 1968.
11. Grimby, G., and Saltin, B. Physiological Analysis of Physically Well-Trained Middle-Aged and Old Athletes. *Acta Med. Scand.* Vol. 179, Fasc 5, 1966, pp. 513-25.

12.   Cooper, K. H., Gey, G. O., and Bottenberg, R. A. The Effect of Cigarette Smoking
      on Endurance Performance. *JAMA.* Vol. 203, No. 3, Jan. 15, 1968, pp. 189-92.
13.   Bergstrom, J., and Hultman, E. Muscle Glycogen Synthesis After Exercise: An
      Enhancing Factor Localized to the Muscle Cells in Man. *Nature.* Vol. 210, Apr.
      16, 1966, 309-10.
14.   Balke, B. Experimental Evaluation of Work Capacity as Related to Chronological
      and Physiological Ageing. Civil Aeromedical Research Institute. FAA Oklahoma
      City, Okla., CARI Report 63-18, Sept. 1963.

Does Physical Fitness Belong In the Schools?

CHARLES TOBEY

Physical Fitness is training, not learning, and it therefore does not belong in the education system. This is an opinion that has recently been voiced by some educators, among them, many physical educators. These people argue that only that which has proven to be educational should be included in the educational system. They might claim that training, for strength and endurance could be better accomplished by a horse trainer than by a teacher. Moreover, they might add, physical fitness is of a temporary nature. The benefits only last as long as the training does. Educational benefits should have a more lasting effect.

Should schools and colleges assume a responsibility for increasing overall capacities in strength, endurance, and speed? Should there be a major emphasis in physical education programs on increasing levels of what is commonly known as physical fitness?

Background

The last three presidents of the United States have placed great importance on producing higher levels of physical fitness among the school age population. Many people think of physical education as physical fitness training when they support physical education in the schools. Physical educators, however, appear to be divided on the question of just how much emphasis there should be on physical fitness in their programs. Since the leaders of this country and many of the people are actively supporting physical fitness programs, it is essential for the physical education profession to develop a stand on this issue and assume leadership in an area of decision making that is going to determine the very nature of physical education programs in the future.

Definitions

There are two commonly accepted definitions of physical fitness which have a direct bearing on resolving this issue. One school of physical educators defines fitness as the capacity to perform a given motor task. This group defines fitness in very specific terms. Physical fitness, for them, is the capacity to do such things as run, jump, dodge, climb, swim, lift weights, or carry loads. Fitness for one activity, however, does not necessarily transfer, with any degree of efficiency to any of the other activities. According to this school of thought, an effort to improve general levels of physical fitness would be wasteful and inefficient, because fitness must be geared to some specific activity to be most useful to the individual.

Another group of physical educators defines fitness in more general terms. For them, fitness denotes a state of being that enables one to participate in all normal activities of life, as well as most emergencies. Fitness, to this group, means fitness for life, and this is the group that has received great support from influential people not directly involved in the field of physical education. John F. Kennedy, in an article for *Sports Illustrated* entitled "The Soft American," stated,

> " . . . physical fitness is not only one of the most important keys to a healthy body; it is the basis of dynamic and creative intellectual activity." Kennedy went on to say that without physical fitness "we will undermine our capacity for thought, for work, and for the use of those skills vital to an expanding and complex America."[1]

This latter concept seems to lend support to a position that fitness, in general, is a worthwhile goal of education.

Others support the development of general levels of fitness as a goal of public schools because of the importance of fitness to an individual's health. Drs. Paul Dudley White and Howard P. Sprague noted heart specialists, give evidence that physical fitness can prolong one's life.[2] Jean Mayer, the famous nutritionist tells how fitness can cut down on "creeping" overweight,[3] and Dr. W. C. Menninger, of the Menninger Clinic, relates physical fitness to sound mental health.[4]

Three Views

Thus, there appears to be three distinct positions on the issue of how much emphasis physical fitness should have in the schools:

1. Fitness is training, not learning, and therefore does not really belong in the educational system. There should be little

---

[1]Kennedy, John F., "The Soft American," *Sports Illustrated,* Dec. 26, 1960, pp. 15-23.
[2]Presentation at a meeting of the Trustees of the California State College on July 13, 1962 by Dr. Raymond A. Snyder, Prof. of Physical Education, University of California at Los Angeles.
[3]Ibid.
[4]Ibid.

emphasis on fitness, or only as much emphasis as is absolutely essential to the performance of skills being taught.

2. Fitness is highly specific. There should be no emphasis on producing general levels of physical fitness in the schools. There can be, however, emphasis on specific fitnesses geared to the performance of specific tasks.

3. General levels of fitness are essential to both the individual's and society's needs and therefore should be emphasized in the schools.

Discussion

In answer to the first position, that fitness is training and not learning, it could be said that physical fitness can be educational if those who teach it want to make it educational. Conversely any skill can be taught through a strict training or conditioning technique that requires the learner to use a minimum of creativity on insight. But, this latter condition need not be the cause. The reasons for learning something, the effects, both physical and psychological, upon the learner, and application of the subject to other areas of life could all be discussed and discovered. This is true for a reading skill as well as for a physical fitness exercise. The task could be as "educational" as the teacher would like it to be. This has implications for the length of the effect of physical fitness on students. If students understand the importance of why they are doing something, it is hoped they will continue to use the skill in later life. This is all we can hope for in any area of subject matter. Without this understanding, the effect would, no doubt, be short lived.

In answer to the second position, that the most effective forms of fitness are highly specific in their nature, I believe that most people still want to be physically fit in general and not necessarily for one specific task. The evidence is fairly conclusive that it is best to wrestle if one wants to be fit for wrestling and best to play lots of tennis if one wants to be fit for tennis. Chin-ups, push-ups, and sit-ups are not the most efficient way to improve one's fitness to wrestle or play tennis. However, most people are not Olympic athletes, nor even varsity athletes, and so are not training for any one sport. If the average individual were asked to pin down exactly what it was he wanted to be fit for, he would find it difficult if not impossible to do so. The average person wants to participate in a variety of activities or tasks.

All-around training that gives equally extensive exercises to develop strength, endurance, and speed, would be best for overall development.[5] A program that included running, weight lifting,

[5]Morehouse, Laurence D. and Miller, Augustus T., *Physiology of Exercise,* The C. V. Mosby Company, St. Louis, p. 261.

circuit training and vigorous games such as handball, squash, and basketball could help to accomplish this purpose of overall fitness. True, this would not be the most efficient way to develop fitness for any specific task, but it is not for one specific task that most individuals are interested in becoming fit. It has become conventional for physical educators to ask the question, fit for what? The answer is for most people, fit for life.

Concluding Statement

Physical fitness is important to an individual's physical and mental health. Physical fitness on a national scale may be necessary to the survival of society. Physical fitness can be educational. It can have permanent benefits, and for most people, should be general, not specific. Physical fitness is essential. Physical fitness belongs in our schools.

CHAPTER III
THE TOTAL CURRICULUM

Quality Physical Education—
a School Responsibility
CHARLES B. WILKINSON

Education, like most human decisions, is a problem of priorities. In assessing their various responsibilities, not enough schools and administrators, and not nearly enough school boards, have recognized the vital importance of quality health-education and physical-education programs. I would like to sell you on the importance of this part of the school curriculum.

For as long as I have been acquainted with education, we have talked in terms of the whole child. I don't think anybody questions the validity of the statement, but, practically speaking, do we mean it? In a cursory examination of physical education, we find we don't. Fewer than 5 percent of the elementary schools in this nation have a gymnasium. Fewer than 14 percent of the secondary schools offer any instruction in the so-called "carry-over" sports. While we may have health courses, it is obvious that they have not been motivating enough to convince some students that they should practice the principles taught.

We must face the fact that we are physical beings, and that our intellectual ability and our intellectual performance are based totally on our good health, vigor, and vitality. Dr. David Henry, president of the University of Illinois, has said:

> The premise that physical vitality promotes intellectual vitality and contributes to academic performance as well as emotional stability is one that every school should embrace and implement. The notion that physical well-being will take care of itself among young people or that intellectual vitality is something apart from good health can no longer be tolerated as an institutional attitude in view of the overwhelming scientific evidence on the subject.

Physical fitness is analogous to a simple tripod—the three legs are a proper amount of rest; an adequate, well-balanced diet; and sufficient exercise. In our society we have severe problems in the areas of diet and exercise.

The problem, of course, is one of motivating the individual, and motivation can be achieved only through good instruction. What the

40

schools are able to do will depend on the value placed on this area of the curriculum.

Poor programs, I feel, have been caused to a degree by varsity athletics. I am totally supportive of varsity athletics, and I do not feel that it has to be an either/or situation—that you cannot have good health education and physical education and good intramural programs and also have good varsity programs. However, concentration on varsity athletics has allowed, unknowingly perhaps, those responsible for school programs to let this substitute for what should be done for the other children in the school.

The program in health and physical education should be compulsory, for the people who need it most are not the most likely to volunteer. At the outset they will not have good coordination and will not do physical things well. They feel embarrassed and won't want to participate, but we must remember that these children will function as adults as well as their health and physical vigor permit. If education does not condition people for the world they will actually be involved in, it has failed to meet its responsibilities.

A good program of health and physical education would include adequate continuing health examinations for every child, with dental and medical care provided to remedy deficiencies; basic developmental programs to bring each child up to an adequate level of strength, coordination, and flexibility; instruction in the lifetime sports so that each person will have a skill in sports (hopefully a variety of skills) that he can use throughout his life. Excellent condition can be achieved through calisthenics, but I have never known anybody who maintained physical fitness by calisthenics alone throughout life, because they become boring.

The Lifetime Sports Foundation has this philosophy: People enjoy playing games if they play them well enough to derive satisfaction instead of frustration. The key to avoiding frustration is good instruction at an age when the muscles are easy to teach, during the school years. Through kinesthetic memory, which everyone possesses, a physical skill once learned is lasting. If you ever learned to ride a bike, 40 years can go by without riding, but you can still get on and ride again. The same is true of swimming, skating, bowling, tennis, and golf.

Whether the lifetime sports skills will be taught, however, remains a question of the priority placed on this area. School board members and educators should take a realistic look at the curriculum in health and physical education, recognizing the basic, fundamental importance of quality instruction that will be motivating for the future living habits of students.

Recent Developments
in Mind-Body Relationships

JOSEPH J. GRUBER AND A. H. ISMAIL

The concept of integrated development or the inter-relatedness of development as proposed by Cowell (1) holds that man's performances in life are a function of his physical, social, emotional and intellectual resources. Each part of the total will not only play its unique role in an act of man, but will also be influenced to a degree by the quality and quantity of the other trait experiences. Hence, one part may exert more influence than the others depending on the nature of the act.

At this time, the writers will confine the following remarks to two parts of the integrated whole, namely, motor and intellectual performance; or the problem of mind-body relationship.

Physical Education in the Past

A quick review of the history of physical education reveals that little attention has been paid to this relationship until relatively recent times (2). Primitive societies practiced activity for survival and religious purposes. In other early cultures such as Egypt, China, India, and Persia, physical education was intended for military, religious, and entertainment purposes. Again, we find the Spartans interested in military proficiency.

On the other hand, it was the Athenian Greeks who stressed development of individual qualities through the physical. However, the times did not as yet recognize a mind-body relationship as revealed in a statement by Socrates: "Why, even in the process of thinking, in which the use of the body seems to be reduced to a minimum, it is a matter of common knowledge that grave mistakes can often be traced to bad health." Plato spoke of healthy bodies for healthy minds. Thus it appears that both elements are recognized by Plato but as separate, independent parts.

The early Christian ascetics of the Dark Ages were opposed to bodily exercise, comfort, or hygiene. During medieval times, physical education's purposes again were moral and physical. The concept of scholasticism also held no room for physical education since all education was supposed to be wholly intellectual in nature.

The Sense Realists of the 17th and 18th century argued for the development of the faculties of both mind and body. Rousseau was the first educational theorist to consider education of the mind and body as being so nearly the same thing. Rousseau's idea was education for the continual growth of an indivisible entity, from birth until death (2).

Learning Through the Senses

Psychologists studying children indicate that the child's first learning experiences come through the senses—touch, taste, smell, seeing, hearing, and feeling. Later they begin to explore the world around them by identifying or relating their body and its parts to objects in space. These explorations when successful develop in the child a sense of satisfaction in that through his body he has been able to communicate; to experience certain physical pleasures; to become familiar with and to control certain movement possibilities of the body which brings satisfaction to him. All contribute to a desirable "body image" or basic self-concept (3).

This foundation is thought to be essential for further learning potential through movement. In short, physical movement becomes the earliest medium for social interaction, personality structure, and the abstract reasoning associated with the creativity of new play experiences. Perhaps this is why many childhood tests of mental ability are heavily loaded with test items that challenge certain sensory-motor mechanisms while presented in a simulated play situation (4).

Some Contemporary Theories

A survey of related twentieth century theories is of prime importance. One is the organismic age theory of Olson (5) which proposed that the performance of a child is associated with certain factors closely related to the total motor, emotional, social, and intellectual development. Each child is to be considered as a whole —an integrated being in developing programs suited to meeting his needs. This concept is proposed for both normal and retarded children.

Another theory is offered by Doman and Delacato (6, 7). This emphasizes the need for neurological organization, which, in normal children is the result of uninterrupted ontogenetic development. Therefore, in treating the retarded, they advocate the neural patterns omitted during neurological development of the child be introduced to him in order to compensate for these missing links. Physical activity is the prescribed therapy medium. However, no experimental evidence is offered that physical activity is more beneficial than another approach.

A third theory, the Perceptual-Motor concept by Kephart (8) stresses the complete perceptual-motor development, which explains learning difficulties as a result of a "breakdown" in the perceptual-motor development of the child.

These theories stress that body and mind are not independent. Such subdivision is arbitrary and completely unfounded. Although much remains to be learned about the brain and central nervous system, neurologists in general agree that the idea of two lives, somatic and psychic, has outlived its usefulness. The psychosomatic concept of medicine recognizes the fact of biological integration and acknowledges its significance.

Experts in physical education and recreation also believe that we perceive and transmit information to the brain with all of our senses. Steinhaus (9) calls our attention to the fact that the most important sense organ in the body is muscle tissue since some forty percent of the axons in the motor-nerve to a muscle are actually sensory fibers that carry impulses to the brain. Hence, through a great deal of our body weight, information from the outside world serving as "neural information" is transmitted to the center of memory, concept formation, thinking, and reasoning. It has been shown in a simple demonstration that thinking of moving one's arm has resulted in recording simple arm muscle twitches on an oscilloscope.

Perhaps at this point a brief review of some of the completed research will help explain in part the validity of these theories. Olson had proposed the Organismic Age concept which really is a composite of mental age, dental age, reading age, weight age, height age, carpal age, and grip age. It is interesting to note that the type of physical items included are essentially growth and strength items.

Olson and Hughes (5) reported some success in predicting achievement from a total organismic age score. Klausmeier, Beeman, and Lehman (10) studied the efficiency of organismic age in predicting language and arithmetic achievement. The variables included were height, weight, grip strength, dental age, carpal age, mental age (California Test of Mental Maturity), and achievement tests in reading, arithmetic, and language. It was concluded that the five physical measures in organismic age contributed little to mental and academic achievement scores.

Other investigators (11, 12, 13, 14) also reported low correlations between growth items such as age, height, weight, grip strength, speed, etc., and intellectual performance. Psychologists now were concluding that there is no substantial relationship between mental and motor performance. These conclusions were presented in the literature for years.

The Concept of Inter-related Development

Stimulated by the tremendous impetus given to physical education and recreation for both normal and retarded children in recent years, researchers began to take a second look at the mind-body problem. This is only appropriate since most of the proposed "special education" programs were based in part on some sort of perceptual-motor theory previously mentioned.

A number of factor analytic studies of researchers now revealed that the concept of inter-relatedness of development has validity. Berry (15) identified two factors that he named *self-inflicted discomfort* and *assertion by power* factors. In the *self-inflicted discomfort* factor, grade point average had a high factor loading along with other motor performance items. In the *assertion by power* factor, grade point average had a high loading along with assertion, self-sentiment, and motor items. These two factors present scientific evidence as to the relationships between academic success, physical performance, and selected personality components. Ismail, Kephart and Cowell (16) found coordination and balance items loading on an *academic development* factor.

Further Evidence on Inter-relatedness

Ismail and Gruber (17) in an extensive series of sequential studies conducted in four cities on fifth- and sixth-grade children provide us with more scientific evidence as to the relationship between mind and body. The rest of this paper is to be devoted to briefly describing the results of these studies and their implications for educators.

These investigators (17) identified 42 items which authorities claimed to measure motor and intellectual powers. Correlation coefficients were computed between these variables for the total group, boys, girls, high, low, and medium achievers. Brief conclusions pertaining to the matrices of intercorrelations are as follows:

A. Growth items (ht., wt.,) are not significantly related to intelligence and academic achievement—except for age.

B. Speed, strength, power and accuracy items are generally not related to intelligence or academic achievement.

C. Coordination items are related to intelligence and academic achievement.

D. Balance and kinesthetic items are related to intelligence and academic achievement to a higher degree in girls than in boys.

E. The coefficients for boys and girls are not in conflict—they tend to go in the same direction and have the same general magnitude indicating stability in the coefficients reported.

F. The correlated variables, their magnitude and direction of relationships lose stability when dividing the group into high, medium and low achievers.

All correlation matrices were submitted to Factor Analysis. This is a multivariate statistical technique which identifies those components or basic factors that are present in a large number of items that authorities claim measure a certain domain. This technique in essence identifies the common elements found in the 42 test items used to measure motor and intellectual performance, and those items that belong to each element or factor.

These factor elements or test items all have something in common with or share part of the information associated with naming each factor. When looking at the tables of factor structure for the total group, boys and girls, one factor is present in all groups—an *Academic Development factor.* Test items that are highly important in naming this factor are I.Q., reading, and arithmetic achievement scores. Other items that share something in common with this factor were balance and coordination items. It is also interesting to note that one of the factors identified for girls was a *Coordination of Lower Limbs factor*—intellectual achievement items were also important in this factor.

In the high achievers we identified a *Mental and Motor Aptitude factor* since measures of I.Q., coordination, balance, and a shuttle run were all important measures of the factor. In medium achievers an *Academic Development factor* appeared that included measures of coordination items, I.Q., and academic achievement scores. This same factor as well as another, namely, *Mental and Motor Aptitude factor,* was found in the low achievers. Thus, scientific evidence is available that indicates measures of academic achievement and motor aptitude are probably tapping some common mode of behavior.

The next stage of the study had to do with developing thirty-six multiple regression equations to predict I.Q. and academic achievement in the total group, boys, girls, high, medium, and low achievers. The multiple correlations ranged from .92 to .62. Hence, it could be concluded that it is possible to predict I.Q. scores and reading and arithmetic scores from a Motor Aptitude Test battery for certain groups; whereas the remaining groups can be classified into a level of achievement based on these regression equations. These motor aptitude test batteries meet one important criterion, namely, they appear to be "culture free" or "culture fair" tests.

The motor aptitude test batteries have several advantages. Some of these advantages are: (1) the tests are nonverbal in nature; (2) they are not associated with undesirable emotional set which is usually present with paper and pencil testing; (3) they do not depend on a person's ability to use paper, pencil or draw something designated by a tester; and (4) they promote a healthy testing atmosphere since the tests are administered in a play situation.

Determining Relative Importance of Items

The next stage of the study dealt with determining the relative importance of growth items, strength items, balance items, and coordination items in predicting intellectual achievement. In order to fulfill the above objective the total amount of information or variance accounted for by each prediction equation was computed. The items associated with coordination and balance were eliminated, one group of items at a time. The amount of information accounted for by the new sub-set of items was obtained. Next both balance and coordination items were eliminated leaving only growth items, strength and kinesthetic items in the prediction scheme.

Hence, from the amount of information lost or reduced by eliminating a set of items, we were able to determine what types of items are more important in the prediction scheme. In general, it was found that the best predictors of Otis I.Q. and Stanford Academic Achievement scores were coordination items, balance items, and growth items in that order for the total group, boys, girls, high, medium and low achievers. Speed, power and strength items apparently have low predictive power for estimating intellectual achievement.

These findings substantiated the earlier work of educational psychologists when they concluded that growth items and strength items added little to the prediction of academic achievement. However, earlier investigators failed to include the coordination, balance and kinesthetic items that probably required cognition for execution in their research designs.

Effect of Organized Physical Education

Until now we have been discussing the relationships that exist between motor and intellectual achievement. However, these relationships do not imply cause and effect. Thus, an experiment was conducted to determine the effect of an organized physical education program on intellectual performance. An experimental group of fifth and sixth graders received 30 minutes of organized physical education instruction three times a week for one school year. The control group of fifth and sixth graders received a daily recess period which is passed off as physical education in many schools. Both groups were equated at the start of the experiment on the criterion measures, namely Otis I.Q. and Stanford Academic Achievement scores.

At the end of the school year the following results were obtained: (1) There were no significant differences in I.Q. scores when comparing the experimental and control group; and (2) there were significant differences in academic achievement in favor of the group receiving the experimental physical education program. The experimental children were three to five months more advanced than the control group in terms of reading and arithmetic achievement (17).

Rutherford (18) in a study on preschool boys and girls compared the recess period with organized P.E. The physical education group again had significantly higher scores in reading readiness tests at the end of the study when compared with the "free play" period.

The results of these studies should clearly demonstrate that the use of recess as a substitute for an organized physical education program in the elementary grades is inexcusable. We must educate principals and administrators that recess periods do not provide the environment that stimulates academic achievement. Nor does the recess period provide instruction in those activities and concepts that will prevent degenerative cardio-vascular disease and at the same time prepare one for leisure living.

Thus, we now have sufficient experimental evidence to permit our physical education objective of Interpretive and Intellectual development to come into its own.

Implications for Future

The implications of these studies on our future programs in teaching and research are worthy of mention. We must determine why the organized physical education class caused improvement in academic achievement. In all probability we should consider the following questions:

A. Did the instruction in organized physical education classes and in arithmetic and reading classes challenge the same neural mechanisms that govern learning?

B. Is all learning basically perceptual-motor in nature? Do we learn with all of our senses in all situations?

C. Was improvement due to achieving success and satisfaction in play that acted as a carry-over motivating device in the school room?

D. Was improvement due to the child's interpretation or thinking through the motor performance and the analysis of instructions presented by the teacher?

E. Was improvement due to teacher-pupil personality interaction?

The answers to these questions will have import in terms of curriculum construction in physical education and recreation for both normal and retarded children.

These studies that we have briefly summarized should be repeated on retarded children. Next steps must be experimental research with various curriculum proposals. We are currently doing many things in our programs for the retarded as well as normals that are not based on science. We have, under the pressures of numbers of pupils to be served and government financing, been stimulated to develop a shotgun curriculum—include a little bit of everything, modify it to the nature of the learner, and in final analysis, hope that some of it hits home. Of course, this is better than nothing, but it is not our best. I am sure that we all agree that our pupils deserve the best that we can provide them.

REFERENCES

1. Cowell, Charles C., and France, Wellman L., *Philosophy and Principles of Physical Education* (Englewood Cliffs, N.J.: Prentice-Hall, Inc., 1963).
2. Van Dalen, D. B., Mitchell, E., and Bennett, B., *A World History of Education* (Englewood Cliffs, N.J.: Prentice-Hall, Inc., 1953).
3. Johnson, Warren R., "Critical Periods, Body Image, and Movement Competency in Childhood," *A Report-Symposium on Integrated Development* (Lafayette, Indiana: Purdue University, June, 1964).
4. Horrocks, John E., *Assessment of Behavior* (Columbus, Ohio: Charles E. Merrill Books, Inc., 1964).
5. Olson, W. C., *Child Development* (Boston: D. C. Heath, 1959).
6. Delacato, Carl H., *The Diagnosis and Treatment of Speech and Reading Problems* (Springfield, Ill.: Charles C. Thomas, 1963).
7. Doman, Glenn, Lecture given at the Institute for the Advancement of Human Potential, January 10, 1966.
8. Kephart, Newell C., *The Slow Learner in the Classroom* (Columbus, Ohio: Charles E. Merrill Books, Inc., 1960).
9. Steinhaus, Arthur, "The Role of Motor Activity in Mental and Personality Development," *A Report-Symposium on Integrated Development* (Lafayette, Indiana: Purdue University, June, 1964).
10. Klausmeier, H. J., Beeman, A., and Lehman, I. J., "Comparisons of Organismic Age and Regression Equations in Predicting Achievement in Elementary School," *Journal of Educational Psychology,* Vol. 49 (August, 1958), pp. 182-186.
11. Bloomers, C., Knief, L. M., and Strand, J. B., "The Organismic Age Concept," *Journal of Educational Psychology,* Vol. 46 (June, 1955), pp. 142-150.
12. Goetzinger, Cornelius P., "A Re-Evaluation of Health Rail-Walking Test," *Journal of Educational Research,* Vol. 54 (1961), pp. 187-191.
13. Klausmeier, H. J., Feldhusen, J., and Check, J., *An Analysis of Learning Efficiency in Arithmetic of Mentally Retarded Children in Comparison with Children of Average and High Intelligence* (Madison, Wisconsin: School of Education, University of Wisconsin, August, 1959).
14. Klausmeier, H. J., "Physical, Behavioral, and Other Characteristics of High and Lower Achieving Children in Favored Environments," *Journal of Educational Research,* Vol. 51 (1958), pp. 573-582.
15. Barry, Alan J., "A Factorial Study of Motivation, Physical Fitness, and Academic Achievement in College Freshmen." Unpublished materials, University of Illinois, Champaign-Urbana, Illinois, 1961.
16. Ismail, A. H., Kephart, N., and Cowell, C. C., "Utilization of Motor Aptitude Test Batteries in Predicting Academic Achievement," *Technical Report No. 1, Purdue University Research Foundation, P. U. 879-64-838,* Lafayette, Indiana, 1963.
17. Ismail, A. H., and Gruber, J. J., *Integrated Development: Motor Aptitude and Intellectual Performance* (Columbus, Ohio: Charles E. Merrill Books, Inc., 1967).
18. Rutherford, W. L., "Perceptual-Motor Training and Readiness." Unpublished paper, Tarkio College, Tarkio, Missouri, 1967.

Health, Physical Education, and Academic Achievement

CHARLES A. BUCHER

Although nine-year-old Susan has normal intelligence, she couldn't master the fundamentals of arithmetic, social studies, English, and writing, regardless of how hard she tried. Her academic difficulties were compounded by a partial paralysis of the right side of her body. After her parents and teachers had unsuccessfully tried everything they could think of to help her, she was referred to the Achievement Center for Children at Purdue University, where much research has been done on children with academic difficulties.

At the Center Susan spent two and a half years in a specially designed program of motor activity under skilled leadership. As a result, her academic and physical improvement was termed "miraculous" by her mother, the principal, and her classroom teacher. Her report card jumped two letter grades in every school subject, and for the first time she was able to participate in a full schedule of classroom activities.

Susan is just one of numerous boys and girls, most of whom do not have a physical handicap like hers, who have been helped to improve academically at the Center by taking part in a program of motor activities used as an integral part of a perceptual-motor training program.

More research is needed to establish and define the exact relationship of physical activity, motor skills, and health to academic achievement, but the evidence to date firmly establishes the fact that a close affinity exists. Indeed, the kind of physical and health education programs which lead to improved physical and social fitness and health are vital to the education and academic achievement of every boy and girl.

This fact has been recognized throughout history by some of the world's most profound thinkers. For example, Socrates stressed that poor health can contribute to grave mistakes in thinking. Comenius noted, "Intellectual progress is conditioned at every step by bodily vigor. To attain the best results, physical exercise must accompany and condition mental training." Rousseau observed that "an enfeebled body enervates the mind" and included a rich program of physical activities for *Emile.*

More recently, such authorities as Arnold Gesell, Arthur T. Jersild, and the Swiss psychologist Jean Piaget found that a child's earliest learnings are motor (involving neuromuscular systems and resulting in movement such as running, jumping, reaching, etc.) in nature and form the foundation for subsequent learnings.

As D. H. Radler and Newell C. Kephart wrote in their authoritative book, *Success Through Play:* "Motor activity of some kind underlies all behavior including higher thought processes. In fact any behavior ... can function no better than do the basic motor abilities upon which it is based."

Physical education, as defined in this article, refers to more than athletics for physically gifted boys and girls. It refers to an instructional program built around basic motor activities which help achieve the goal of physical, emotional, and mental well-being for every student. School health programs are concerned with the modification of behavior and the imparting of scientific health knowledge leading to the same goals, together with provisions for health services and a healthful physical and emotional environment.

Academic achievement refers to the progress a child makes in school as measured by his scores on achievement tests, his grade-point averages, his promotion from grade to grade, and the development of proper attitudes. As any experienced teacher knows, academic achievement requires more than intellectual capacity. Nonintellectual factors, such as the will to achieve, health, and self-concept, are almost certain to play an important part in a student's ability to achieve academically.

Health and physical education programs are related to academic achievement in at least four ways: (a) through emphasis on the development of motor skills, (b) by promoting physical fitness, (c) by imparting knowledge and modifying behavior in regard to good health practices, and (d) by aiding in the process of social and emotional development which leads to a more positive self-concept.

Typical of the research studies confirming the relationship between motor skills and academic achievement is that of G. L. Rarick and Robert McKee who studied 20 third graders grouped according to whether they had high or low motor proficiency. The study showed that the group with high motor proficiency had a greater number who achieved "excellent" or "good" ratings in reading, writing, and comprehension than the group with low motor efficiency.

In another study, Jack Keogh and David Benson experimented with the motor characteristics of 43 underachieving boys, ages 10 to 14, enrolled in the Psychology Clinic School at UCLA. They found that as individuals, half of the boys from 10 to 12 years old exhibited poor motor performance.

A. H. Ismail, N. Kephart, and C. C. Cowell, utilizing motor aptitude tests, found that IQ and academic success could be predicted from these tests, with balance and coordination items the best predictors for estimating achievement.

Other studies indicate that the child's first learnings accrue from an interaction with his physical and social environment. Physical action provides the experience to clarify and make meaningful concepts of size, shape, direction, and other characteristics. In addition, through physical activities he experiences sensations, he has new feelings, and he develops new interests as well as satisfies old curiosities.

The importance of physical fitness was stressed by Lewis Terman more than twenty-five years ago. After working with gifted children he stated, "Results of physical measurements and medical examinations provide a striking contrast to the popular stereotype of the child prodigy, so commonly depicted as a pathetic creature, an overserious, undersized, sickly, bespectacled child." He went on to say that physical weakness was found nearly 30 percent fewer times in children of higher intelligence than in those of lower intelligence. Many research studies since Terman have supported the contention that physical fitness is related to academic achievement.

H. H. Clarke and Boyd O. Jarman, in a study of boys, 9, 12, and 15 years old, found a consistent tendency for the high groups on various strength and growth measures to have higher means on both academic achievement tests and grade-point averages than low groups. Studies conducted at the universities of Oregon and Iowa and at Syracuse and West Point have shown a significant relationship between physical fitness and academic success and between physical fitness and leadership qualities. David Brace, F. R. Rogers, Clayton Shay, Marcia Hart, and others have done extensive research showing relationships between scholastic and academic success and physical fitness.

A good school health program, too, makes a definite contribution to good scholarship. In health education classes, students learn about the harmful effects of alcohol, smoking, and dangerous drugs; they obtain scientifically accurate information about such things as good nutrition, the requisites for good vision, the importance of exercise, and the ingredients for healthful personality development and mental health.

Through the development of desirable attitudes and the application of health knowledge, the student achieves his maximum strength, energy, endurance, recuperative power, and sensory acuity. Furthermore, the effective school health program helps boys and girls to understand and appreciate the value of good health as a means of achieving their greatest productivity, effectiveness, and happiness as individuals.

Some research has shown a relationship between scholastic success and the degree to which a student is accepted by his peer group. Similarly, the boy or girl who is well grounded in motor skills usually possesses social status among his or her peers.

For example, J. B. Merriman found that such qualities as poise, ascendancy, and self-assurance were significantly more developed in students of high motor ability than in those with low motor ability.

Other research shows that popularity in adolescent boys is more closely associated with physical and athletic ability than with intelligence; that leadership qualities are most prevalent among school boys (and West Point cadets) who score high on physical fitness tests; and that well-adjusted students tend to participate to a greater extent in sports than poorly adjusted students.

Physical education and health not only affect social development but emotional development as well. Games provide release from tension after long periods of study; furthermore, achievement in physical activities gives students a sense of pride which pays dividends in emotional satisfaction and well-being.

In this sense, the value of physical education and health may be greater for educationally subnormal students than for average boys and girls. James N. Oliver, lecturer in education at the University of Birmingham, England, has done much research on educationally subnormal boys and has found that systematic and progressive physical conditioning yields marked mental and physical improvement. He believes such improvement resulted from the boys' feelings of achievement and of consequent improved adjustment.

The value of physical education and health programs will depend largely upon whether or not they meet the following criteria:

The physical education program includes a variety of daily movement experiences and instruction in many basic motor activities, aimed not at making the student a superior performer in one or two, but stressing a modest performance in all, consistent with his developmental level. It also helps each student to achieve physically according to desirable standards.

The health program provides boys and girls with accurate and significant health knowledge related to their individual needs and interests. There is also concern for health services and a healthful physical and emotional environment.

Physical education and health programs are accorded educational respectability so that students and parents will more readily appreciate their value and seek the benefits they offer.

By providing these essentials, the school will help to ensure a high standard of academic achievement on the part of all boys and girls.

Physical Education and Recreation as Adjuncts to the Education of the Mentally Retarded

JULIAN U. STEIN

The President's Council on Physical Fitness has recommended strongly that all children participate in vigorous physical activity every day. The Council has further emphasized the need for the diagnosis of the physically underdeveloped and impaired and the institution of appropriate remedial programs. Today many mentally retarded youngsters would also have to be classified as physically underdeveloped.

Parents, the interested lay public, special interest groups, and a few dedicated professionals are doing something about meeting the growing need for physical education and recreation for the retarded. From Boston to Miami, New York to Los Angeles, St. Paul to Nashville something is being done; in rural communities and in large urban centers programs are being developed. Physical education is being recognized for the contributions it can make to the total growth and development of the retarded; recreation is being looked upon for its educational impact and potential for the retarded. Camping programs for the retarded are growing in number; year around recreation is on the upswing; and residential facilities are expanding their formal and informal physical education and recreation programs. Much more is being done for the retarded in these areas around the country than is generally known.

The Situation

In spite of growing interest and increasing number and quality of programs for the retarded, the generally prevailing situation is one of inactivity, lack of opportunity, and little participation by the retarded in school physical education and community recreation programs. In many communities offerings are simply of a token nature to appease parental and community special interest groups. Unhappily too few colleges and universities are even acquainting their physical education and recreation major students with the characteristics and needs of the retarded. When young men and women take their first jobs and are there confronted by retarded youngsters, many of them are frightened because of lack of knowledge and understanding about the retarded—scared into an ostrich-like approach, hoping that by ignoring the problem it will go away.

But this won't happen. These children are in our schools, on our playgrounds, and coming to us in ever increasing numbers. Public education and community recreation are falling heir to increasing numbers of mentally retarded. Medical technology is enabling many babies to survive infancy where so many died in the past. Changing philosophies and principles are evolving wherein the retarded are whenever possible kept in the home and in the community rather than being institutionalized. In many areas public education and municipal recreation are assuming responsibility for the trainable as well as the educable retarded. And, through the efforts of special interest groups and the zeal of a few individuals, physical education and recreation are being recognized as potent tools in the education and training of the retarded.

The Individual

The retarded are imbued with the same basic needs and drives, and require the same satisfactions for a happy adjustment in our society as do their non-retarded contemporaries. In addition to the fulfillment of these basic needs, the retarded must also overcome the obstacles brought about by retardation as they strive for maximum degrees of independence. In their quest to prepare retarded children to take their rightful place in our society, many teachers have given disproportionate amounts of time and placed too great emphasis upon the academic aspects of the program. As a result little time or opportunity has been left for exploration of activities of a recreational nature that will contribute to the total growth and development of the mentally retarded. Insufficient time and opportunity have been given to expand interests and to capitalize on special abilities that will enable the retarded to live fuller, richer, and even more productive lives.

So much of one's success today is determined by his ability to understand and manipulate verbal symbols. Because by their nature the retarded are nonverbal, many have known nothing but failure and frustration as they have wrestled with the abstractions of programs in which success is determined by academic ability. Programs and activities in which the retarded can express himself in nonverbal but concrete, symbolic, and meaningful ways take on even greater meaning in this condition which manifests itself in poor learning, inadequate social adjustment, and delayed achievement. Important contributions to emotional and psychological stability are made through the cathartic values of activity and movement. Preparation for future vocational endeavor and for wholesome participation in recreational activities and wise use of leisure time can also be stimulated through such a program.

Coordination

With the recreation and education programs of the retarded properly attuned, the two will supplement and complement each other. Basically the aims of the two programs are identical—to help the retarded achieve the maximum of his individual potential for independence. Fulfillment of this goal will be achieved as the retarded attains abilities and attitudes that enable him to socialize better through improved adjustment to group demands, to exhibit improved self-care habits, to attain higher levels of motor control, proficiency, and coordination, to develop prevocational and vocational skills, to show improved communication skills, and improved educational and intellectual skills and development. In addition, mental health should be furthered through both programs as the retarded gains in feelings of acceptance and confidence, and in the development of greater self-respect and self-image. Social situations and environmental conditions should be carefully controlled according to the retardate's level and potential for social independence. Programs, techniques, and methods will vary from the highly sheltered situation, through lessening degrees of social isolation to partial and eventually total integration in the community's resources for recreation or the school's physical education program.

There is some evidence that with the proper type of stimulation and training a retarded individual may learn to do more complicated things than would be expected on the basis of his mental age. Recent trends in research show that the lack of intellectual ability resulting from arrested mental development need not affect the levels of physical fitness and motor development of the retarded. Based upon the scientific evidence reported to date, certain guideposts can be given concerning the psychomotor function of the mentally retarded:

1. In spite of underachievement with respect to motor function, the mentally retarded are much nearer the norm physically than mentally.
2. Motor function and proficiency can be improved in the retarded as a result of planned and systematic programs of physical education.
3. There are real differences to be expected in working with institutionalized retardates vs. those enrolled in public school special classes.
4. The mentally retarded achieve better in activities characterized by simple rather than complex neuromuscular skills.
5. Achievement in the area of physical fitness development apparently does not result in corresponding differential gains with respect to sociometric status.
6. Significant IQ gains have been demonstrated by educable mentally retarded boys subjected to programs of planned and progressive physical education activities.
7. Motor proficiency and intelligence are more highly correlated in the retarded than in normal children.

Empirical statements from those working directly with retarded children in these programs reinforce these findings:

1. "The teacher is probably most able to reach the retarded in two areas of learning, music and physical education which appear closely related and basic to recreation programs." (Dubin, 1954)

2. "Much improvement was noted in levels of physical fitness and in the development of both basic and specific motor skills. Several of these youngsters (trainable boys and girls) had virtually no verbal communication, but expressed themselves in symbolic and meaningful ways through the movement involved. This was especially evident when basic rhythms and fundamental movement activities with music were used ... Even these youngsters voluntarily participated in a special demonstration night for the P.T.A. All of these children were eager and responsive. However, the younger ones progressed more rapidly and were less reluctant to try some activities. ... " (Stein, 1966)

3. "Students have developed some skills and abilities to rather high degrees of proficiency; all of the boys have progressed tremendously in the direction of physical, emotional, psychological, and social self-sufficiency and self-realization. They have become better adjusted to the school population, and the school population to them." (Stein, 1962)

4. "Yesterday during a visit to Wakefield, I was amazed at the improvement in physical coordination exhibited by the older boys whom I have known for several years. This improvement is obviously the result of the program that you and your successors have followed at Wakefield." (Personal communication from Mr. Henry Gardner, Coordinator of Services for Exceptional Children, Arlington County, Virginia.)

5. "Through participation in a daily program of physical education activities, elementary school retarded boys and girls participated more actively in before and after school physical recreation programs, and attained levels of performance commensurate with their grade peers. This same program provided a stimulus for a variety of other educational experiences of a more academic nature, as well as being psychologically stimulating and emotionally envigorating." (Stein, 1966)

Undoubtedly the progress that has been shown—research and empirical—by mentally retarded subjects who have participated in planned programs of physical education have accrued through the interplay of a complex of factors—achievement and success which for many was the first time they had experienced the satisfaction of even completing a task, improved confidence, better adjustment, a feeling of importance because of the interest and attention centered on them, greater competitive spirit, increased pride, improved physical condition, more perseverance, and increased desire to perform well. With the retarded these factors have even greater meaning and significance than with the normal population.

Concluding Statement

Not only is greater emphasis needed on the physical education and recreational pursuits of the retarded, more time devoted to physical activities, and greater demands made on each of these children, but a much greater percentage of time given to the physical and recreational activities, abilities, interests, and attitudes of the retarded. Utilization of the great variety and diversity of physical and recreational activities can serve as a springboard for success in many areas not heretofore thought within the realm of possibility for the retarded. Teachers and recreation leaders must not be restricted nor limited by convention nor the presentation of watered down programs for normal children as their efforts for the retarded. The potential of recreational and physical activities of all types as a stimulus for greater learning, improved mental health, and greater self-realization has been relatively untapped as a method of educating the retarded at all levels.

In the last few years we have gained theoretical knowledge and practical know-how in developing programs of physical education and recreation for the mentally retarded. We are learning more each day about activities, methods, and techniques and their effects upon the physical, psychological, social, and emotional development of the retarded. While we have a long way to go in our professional pursuit of excellence in programming for the retarded, we have made this start and have shown the importance of physical education and recreation on the team. We solicit your help, your support, and your cooperation as the administrators of our schools and school systems to give us the chance—accept the retarded in your schools, provide personnel to conduct these programs, schedule the retarded for physical education and recreational activities so that they will contribute to their total growth and development, and assist in providing facilities, supplies, and equipment for these programs. Give us the chance and we will help to put the education into physical education for the mentally retarded.

SELECTED REFERENCES
1. DUBIN, H. N. "Some observations on the place of physical education and
    a health program in building a program for the mentally retarded child."
    Amer. J. ment. Defic., 1954, 59, 6-12.
2. STEIN, J. U. "Adapted physical education for the educable mentally
    handicapped." J. hlth. phys. educ. Rec., 1962, 33, 30-31, 50-51.
3. STEIN, J. U. "Physical education and recreation for the mentally
    retarded." Phys. educ. Newsletter, 1966 (spring supplement).

Learning About Movement

NAOMI ALLENBAUGH

Through the decades, elementary physical education has
progressed through three major stages, the major emphases of these
stages being participation, socialization, and physical fitness. A
rapidly developing fourth stage, one of greater sophistication,
combines these three earlier stages and adds an emphasis on
understanding the environment, movement, and man. It focuses on
education for efficiency of movement and for self-discovery,
self-direction, and self-realization while incorporating from the earlier
emphases such specifics as understanding of and improvement in
fundamental and specialized motor skills.

The great increase in knowledge has brought sharply into focus
the need for each child to have a broad understanding of many areas
and how they relate to each other. Physical education, like every
other discipline, can be organized so each child can gradually develop
the main ideas of the discipline through the accumulation,
comprehension, and synthesis of the related subject matter. Let us
examine three of many broad concepts around which it can be
organized: Man moves to survive; man moves to discover and
understand his environment; man moves to control and adjust to his
environment.

The first concept, *man moves to survive,* recognizes the
anatomical and physiological nature of man and his need to acquire
physiological understanding and readiness for efficient movement.
The individual must develop, maintain, and value muscular strength,
endurance, flexibility, agility, and balance if he is to survive without
unusual dependency on others.

Young children force parents and nursery school teachers to
recognize the second concept—*man moves to discover and understand
his environment.* Yet when the elementary school child enters the
gymnasium to participate in physical education, his drive to examine
and explore is frequently destroyed or destructively limited rather
than released, encouraged, and guided. As a child comes to

understand his environment and use it successfully in movement, he acquires a more realistic body image and a more wholesome self-concept. With the resulting sense of power, he can then accept the task of developing his individual potential rather than wastefully trying to imitate other people.

As the understanding of self and environment evolves, the third concept—*man moves to control and adjust to his environment*—takes on deeper meaning for the individual. He begins to recognize that control of and adjustment to the environment is dependent upon efficiency of movement. Thus he begins to work for the advantageous use of the elements of movement—space, time, force, and flow.

For example, he works to develop the ability to apply appropriate force in his movements in relation to the space and time available to him. He works to develop a smoothness, a flow, a unity of all parts of the body involved in movement. He acquires the ability to understand his movement and he learns ways of improving it.

This ability involves the development of a comprehension of the mechanics of motion. His movement leads him to ask:

What is the center of gravity in my body? How does it influence equilibrium? How do I use my body to maintain balance?

How can my arms, my legs, my whole body serve as levers to increase the force and speed with which I move?

To gain an understanding of the principles of movement, he begins to ask: How can I distribute my weight to gain accuracy, force, and speed, yet maintain my balance? Why does continuing movement in the direction of projected or received force increase my efficiency? Why is my whole body involved in effective movement?

In seeking and finding the answers to these questions, he increases the vocabulary from which he can select the movements most effective in meeting specific demands of the moment. In order to choose which movements are appropriate for various activities, he must develop an understanding of efficient performance of locomotor skills (how to walk, run, hop, leap, slide, skip, and perform combinations of these), nonlocomotor skills (turn, twist, stretch, bend, and swing), and manipulative skills (throw, hit, and catch).

Finally he becomes proficient in the *instant organization* of any combination of these skills demanded for an efficient response to a given situation. He uses his movement vocabulary purposefully.

What experiences can the teacher provide to help the child grasp the meaning of the movement concepts just discussed, to develop movement proficiency, and to become a self-accepting, productive individual?

One answer is to have all children working independently but simultaneously to discover the many different ways in which each child can move *within, through,* and *with* his environment and to establish the requisites for effective movement. The teacher can base problems on the elements of movement (space, time, force, and flow) and their various dimensions so the child moves alone or with others or he moves upon, through, around, and with moving or stationary objects.

In solving these problems, the child uses many fundamental motor skills. Sometimes, at a very young age, he will discover and use combinations of movements which in reality are specialized motor skills normally used in the complex organization of a dance, a sport, or a game. The important factor in the use of problems is the emphasis on body movement as it relates to space, time, force, and flow.

ELEMENTS AND DIMENSIONS OF MOVEMENT

Space	Levels: high, medium, low.
	Ranges: wide-narrow, far-near.
	Directions: forward-backward, upward-downward, sideward, circle, diagonal.
	Shapes: Round, straight, angular, twisted.
Force	Heavy-light, strong-weak, tight-loose.
Time	Slow, medium, fast.
Flow	Free, bound, sequential.

BODY FOCUS

Body Relationships	Head or feet above, level with, or below torso, and combinations.
Body Leads	Shoulder, hip, head, knee, foot, etc., combinations.
Body Supports	Feet, knees, hands, back, shoulders, head, etc., combinations.
Body Control	Starts-stops.

The direct teaching of an exact skill may follow these earlier experiences or the problems may be deliberately designed so the exact skill will gradually emerge. Such movement experience allows each child to progress at his own rate and to feel comfortable with the way he moves rather than to be blocked in his initial learning by the necessity to move exactly as the teacher says he must.

Some specific examples of problems developed around the elements and dimensions of space will serve to illustrate the above ideas:

In what different directions can you move (forward, backward, and the like)?

At how many different levels (high, low, medium) can you move: through space, in your own space, in space with an object, through space with an object, with a partner through space, with a partner in your own small space, sending an object through space to a partner, moving yourself through space as you send an object through space to a partner?

How many different ways can you change the width and length of your body (wide to narrow, long to short, and the like)?

What different shapes can you make with your body (round, straight, angular, curled, twisted)?

Problems using the elements of force and time can be developed in a similar manner. Following these experiences, the children can deal with increasingly complex problems, such as combinations of dimensions within an element (high, backward, wide), combinations of dimensions selected from the different elements (high, forward, fast; high, forward, slow; high, backward, fast; high, backward, slow).

In experimenting with such problems, the child experiences contrasts in dimensions and discovers the ease or difficulty of movement inherent in certain combinations. Throughout these experiences the teacher can raise questions to direct pupils' attention to *what* they are doing, *why* some combinations of movements are more difficult than others, *what* is valuable in the movements, and *how* pupils can become more proficient.

Such movement experiences, which lead into fundamental motor skills and then into specialized motor skills, should lead the student to value the concepts of survival, of discovery and control of the environment, and of self.

14

Social Development —
The Forgotten Objective?

JOSEPH B. OXENDINE

Social Development, as an objective of physical education, has fallen into ill repute during the past few years. Recent research, literature, and conference attention have largely ignored this aspect of physical education teaching.

A number of factors have contributed to the recent decline of interest in social efficiency as a major objective of physical education. One important fact has been the focus of attention on the physical fitness objective.

Many physical education teachers have encouraged almost absolute concentration on the physical objective, which has been called our "unique role." Enthusiasm for social development has lessened because "all other teachers do this." Some physical educators simply believe that the fitness and skill objectives are important enough to command their total attention; devoting time to other goals would reduce effectiveness in the primary objective.

In addition, in this age of science, there is a growing intolerance for any claim for which a direct cause and effect relationship has not been clearly demonstrated. This intolerance extends to the point of ignoring the bulk of related evidence and expert opinion. There are also many teachers who are not greatly impressed with an objective which cannot be measured with ease and validity.

An apparent lack of success on the part of some teachers has resulted in their becoming convinced that social development cannot take place in physical education activities. Young teachers are especially apt to discard the idea if their first efforts do not show immediate results. But obvious changes in social attitudes and behavior rarely occur; the seeds of desirable attitudes and behavior take some time to germinate and longer to bear fruit. The speed will depend upon the social climate as well as the receptivity of the individual.

A Reasonable Goal?

Many teachers reject the social objective because they do not believe it is a reasonable goal. They have serious questions about the possibility of significant social development taking place in the school setting. Some of these questions, and a discussion of the answers, are presented here.

Does an individual "learn" leadership, perseverance, ethical character, and other social traits? This question is still seriously asked by some, even though behavioral scientists have long indicated that social traits are learned, not inherited. Anthropologists have described differences in competitive attitude, acceptable moral behavior, and social customs among different cultures. Researchers have clearly shown that preferences for food, practices of neatness, social tolerance, and other social traits can be developed among young people. Therefore, the question as to whether or not social efficiency is learned is no longer a basic one.

Can the school be instrumental in developing these traits? If one accepts the premise that social traits are learned, this leads to other questions, such as when, where, and how does this take place. Of course, all of society teaches the individual. An erroneous tendency is to place absolute responsibility with one aspect of society. Teachers sometimes assume an unresponsible attitude for the social development of children because of the few hours a day spent in school. Parents also claim a limited influence on the child because of their inability to control the outside environment. Religious institutions cannot presume to have complete control over moral attitudes and behavior. Recreational and social agencies have a similar problem. Physical educators indicate that their influence is further limited since the child is six years of age when he enters school, and often thirteen years old or more before he gets into a regular physical education or athletic program.

There is some truth in all of these claims of limited influence. Too often, however, they reflect an effort to evade responsibility. It is true that no one aspect of society has complete influence over the young person. A realistic point of view holds that all youth serving organizations and individuals have some influence on, and therefore some responsibility for, the social development of the child. Teachers, as a part of the total environment, should make their mark. The development of social skills, as well as attitudes and behavior, is possible at any age. Of course, the younger person is more susceptible to social change. It is unrealistic, however, to suggest that the child's personality, character, and social skills are rigidly established at age six, or even at adolescence. The school, while obviously not having a total influence, has quite a large role to play in this part of the child's education.

Can physical education and athletics make a difference in social efficiency? When compared with other phases of the school, physical education and athletics are in a unique position for affecting attitude and behavioral change. The emotional involvement usually associated with these activities and the degree of interaction among students are important for social development.

One's basic attitudes, prejudices, and general social behavior are not easily changed. An emotional as well as an intellectual involvement is usually essential for any change to take place. A purely intellectual approach, with scientific and/or logical persuasion, has serious limitations. Likewise, a purely emotional appeal will not be very influential with reasonably prudent individuals. A combination of the two, with considerable emphasis on personal involvement, is most effective with young people.

Physical education (including regular class, intramural, and varsity programs) represents a phase of the school program about which most of the youngsters get excited. Few other aspects of the school develop as much general interest and enthusiasm among both participants and observers. It is true that a good climate for social change and development might be established in other school activities, such as dramatics, student government, or a debating club. It is conceivable that considerable positive emotional involvement might be associated with a regular class in science, mathematics, or geography. It is safe to assume, though, that physical education and athletics are *usually* most effective in commanding a greater degree of the student's total attention. The inherent and cultural interest in play and sports makes this area an effective climate for social change.

Another favorable feature of the physical education program is that it almost naturally promotes interaction among students. Social growth takes place only when persons communicate, cooperate with, compete against, or in some way relate to others. The teacher-pupil relationship is only a small part of the social setting. Again, one can say, other phases of the school, even a mathematics class, can involve social interaction among pupils. It must generally be admitted, however, that the physical education class or a sports team are more easily adaptable to student communication. Further, the relationships are usually more informal and probably more lifelike than those social situations arranged in the classroom.

Are social skills and attitudes transferred to other areas of the person's life? Present knowledge about transfer indicates that a very high percentage of skills and attitudes will be transferred if the individual sees the relationships or the principles involved. One experiment showed that when children learned neatness habits in one class, these habits were transferred to all areas of the child's school experience. The person who has developed leadership skill and confidence will use them in other situations where the principles apply. It is unlikely that a person who had developed honesty and fair play in a sports activity will violate these characteristics in a classroom examination. Social tolerance and respect gained on an athletic field will most probably carry over to other avenues of one's experience. There is need, however, for the teacher to teach for transfer.

Implications for the
Physical Education Program

If teachers accepted the challenge of social development, what difference would it make in the program? This discussion is not intended to be a detailed blueprint or design for promoting social efficiency in the gymnasium or on the playfield, but a few general suggestions in conclusion may aid in giving direction.

Some teachers and coaches are already concerned with social development and have organized their programs and procedures so that this aim will be accomplished. Others, with relatively slight changes, could greatly increase the possibilities for social growth. It is important to note that the program geared for social development need not reduce the emphasis on physical fitness or skill development.

Very little class time need be devoted to a discussion of social efficiency. Far more important are the organization techniques and climate of the class. The process selected to accomplish physical objectives is the strategic factor in social development. Some discussion or explanation, however, needs to be given to transfer or general application of the principles learned.

The teacher should organize the class into one or more social units. Group action and communication should be promoted. A class in physical education which is dominated by the teacher is no more conducive to social development than the same techniques in the language course. From a social standpoint, a teacher-directed mass drill is little better than a class of one pupil. However, if responsible citizenship roles are encouraged, and if the teacher or coach exhibits a positive example, the physical education or sports experience can be a most dynamic force in the social development of the young person.

SECTION TWO
SOME TEACHING SUGGESTIONS

Introduction To Section II

Although each teacher uses the methods and techniques which provide him with a sense of security and accomplishment, there is much to be said for a philosophy which allows one to try ideas which have been advanced by others.

The material presented in this section encompasses a variety of viewpoints. Each has been found to be workable. The astute reader will be able to think through the various processes and determine which ones may work well for him. Experimentation and modification of those ideas which are not at first accepted will also prove to be beneficial.

CHAPTER IV
PHYSICAL EDUCATION FOR THE TYPICAL CHILD

Making School Learned Physical Education A Continuing Force For Future Fitness
JULIAN A. STEIN

Man is basically an active organism that requires big muscle activity as a part of his daily routine to help sustain the proper physiological, psychological, and emotional balance necessary for a well-rounded life. In days gone by man's way of life insured the necessary physical activity as he carried on his daily tasks in maintaining himself and his family. However, as civilization progressed, and man mastered his environment through science and technology, machines replaced muscle power, initiative gave way to routine, satisfactions of the past gave rise to the stresses of the present, and long hours of labor changed into increased leisure time. More people, working fewer hours per week in more monotonous jobs, became concentrated in large urban population centers. With this trend showing no apparent abatement, the need is even greater for

67

recreational opportunities and services planned and conducted by trained leadership. Many of the skills, attitudes, habits, and knowledge can be matured through physical education programs in our schools and colleges. The pattern in too many communities leads one to ask how much we are preparing our boys and girls for active leisure.

There are many signs of the times which we should heed. A glance at the television guide of any paper reveals programs such as Slimnastics or Jack LaLanne; a look in the local newspaper shows advertisements for health clubs and exercise for physical fitness centers; and, many articles claim that keys to youth and fitness come through special diets, unique exercise programs (including the use of isometrics), and through the use of special equipment such as rowing machines, stationary bikes, and weights. Many of these are "crash" programs that attract individuals who have finally realized that regular and progressive exercise is a necessity for a healthful, wholesome, and meaningful life. Some of these have been awakened through reports of their physicians; others have been influenced by the current literature regarding the importance of fitness and the contribution of activity to its attainment; a few have seen the effects of such participation of their friends or associates. But, how many have been guided into intelligent, continuous, regular, and progressive programs through their school or college physical education experiences? Unfortunately, if we are at all honest, we would have to say that too few cases result from this, and that in many instances our programs may be responsible for the apathy of people to physical activity and their allergy to big muscle activities!

An evaluation of physical education programs might reveal a number of reasons for such situations. There are many factors which could and do influence this—overcrowded classes, little or no classification system, poor progression in activities and skills, little articulation from level-to-level, school-to-school, or grade-to-grade, too much free-play and too little instruction, too much repetition in skills and activities, failure to meet interests, needs, abilities, and limitations of individuals, poor public relations, allowing substitution of other areas for physical education, little direction of programs, poor facilities, and, in general, too little education in physical education. However, in spite of these factors, there is an additional one which has been overlooked for too long!

In our desire to provide activity to meet the current needs, we have failed to show our classes the "why" of such activity, and have left them with no more than a hollow shell for the future. In many cases children have developed a bad taste for Physical Education from their first experiences in the elementary schools. Far too many programs become "ball" centered too early, at a time when the hand-eye coordination is rather poor. Many children have little success in such a program and develop negative attitudes toward it. These attitudes are furthered by those of many adults, and added to through the recognition and attention that those superior in such abilities get through the interscholastic programs (even in some elementary schools). Thus, by the time many children get to the junior and senior high school they are well along the road to being lost. When they come face-to-face with the secondary program, partaking in many activities with no attempt to show their importance, and little effort to develop positive attitudes or regular habits of activity, there is no wonder that many develop an adversity to physical activities.

Might it not be a wise procedure for physical educators to invest some of the activity time of the present to encourage continued activity in the future? Couldn't this be aided through periodic classroom sessions in which many of the "whys" and "wherefores" of physical activity, its importance to one's total well-being, its relationship to a balanced and wholesome life, and how the lack of exercise leads to many physical, psychological, and emotional disturbances? These should be regular sessions (at least twice per month, or possibly even once per week) in which the teacher is well prepared and uses all of the best methods, techniques, materials, and resources available to him. Appropriate assignments, reading, reports, and testing should be included to make this as meaningful an experience as possible.

Such sessions should be supplemented by attempts to stimulate interest in activities that are impractical or impossible to hold within the activity program itself. Movies, film-strips, lectures, resource visitors, reports, and discussions concerning topics such as skiing, ice skating, hunting, fishing, water skiing, camping, cycling, hiking, boating, canoeing, water sports, winter activities, and the like can be made integral parts of the program and can pay great dividends in the future. These sessions could also be beneficial in discussing rules, strategy, fundamentals, and in using audio visual materials for units of instruction within the activity program. This could actually give more time for skill instruction when the classroom sessions are well planned and wisely used.

Since watching sports activities is such a deep-seated part of our culture, the classroom sessions could also be used to help develop greater understanding and appreciation of the games viewed by millions each year in person or on television. Understanding of the basic concepts of the game, offensive and defensive alignments, scoring, strategy, techniques and skills, appropriate spectator behavior, expected codes of sportsmanship, and how to watch the respective sports are but a few of the areas that could be included. Again, the approach must be one of education—well planned and presented. If well done such areas could be among the most beneficial and lasting contributions to physically educating an individual.

In many programs it has been noted that there is little progression in teaching skills and activities, and that many units are so short that they are in fact educationally sterile. These two conditions must be corrected if our programs are to reap their full potential. Programs must be planned and administered so that children will have sufficient time to develop skills that can be used as effective tools for wholesome physical activity in the future. It is a known fact that people pursue activities in which they do well and from which they derive satisfaction. Participation in sports activities in which an individual has little skill results in failure and frustration, and subsequent rejection of the activity. Because so many Americans have not been schooled adequately in these skills, nor have they been endowed with an appreciative attitude toward activities, many have become sedentary at a time when a healthy mind and an alert mind require more and varied activities. It is partly because of our failure that the current "crash" programs have gained such popularity. Are these programs what the American public really wants? Wouldn't activities more consistent with the American philosophy of play and sports be more beneficial and meaningful to all concerned? It seems that it is time that each of us take stock of ourselves and our programs, and make changes where necessary to provide programs that not only meet current needs but make adequate preparation for an active future.

An Emphasis On Elementary School Physical Education—Goal:
A Superior Program For All
John Puckett

In many school systems the secondary school physical education programs receive preference over the elementary school programs in the areas of leadership, equipment and supplies. This indicates that we may be concentrating on the "second floor" and to some extent we may be neglecting the "foundation."

The national government has expressed its concern over the promotion of physical fitness and most state governments have made provisions for physical education in elementary schools. This, however, is not enough. We must improve existing programs if we hope to achieve our recognized objectives in physical education.

The following suggestions are proposed as aids in improving our present elementary school physical education programs:

1. *School Administrators Should Promote and Expect Well-Organized and Well-Supervised Programs of Physical Education in Elementary Schools.* Those school systems which follow a tradition of unsupervised or partially supervised classes of physical education should make every effort to remedy the situation. As in other areas of the school program, the role of leadership lies with the administration.

2. *A Varied Program of Physical Activities Should Be Planned.* The elementary school physical education program should include such activities as tag games, low organized ball games, relays, athletic lead-up games, creative rhythms and dance, singing games, folk dances, stunts and tumbling, and individual and couple activities (3:51).

To prepare prospective elementary school teachers in these areas, at least two semesters or three quarters of professional physical education courses should be required in colleges and universities.

Also, an effective and continuous in-service training program in physical education should be organized. The in-service programs should be based upon the requests of the classroom teachers and they should also have an active part in the presentations.

3. *Physical Education Opportunities Should Be Provided for All Pupils.* With the advice of physicians, individual modified activities should be provided for those pupils with physical defects (2:1). In too many instances, the pupils who most need physical activity are the ones who are excused from all physical education.

In addition to physical education classwork, varied intramural opportunities should be provided for those pupils in the upper elementary grades (4:39).

If interschool athletics are promoted (and whether they should or should not be will be discussed here), this should be done only after a superior program of classroom activities is provided for all pupils. Time, leadership and funds should not be drained from regular class activities in order to make interschool athletics possible.

4. *Fun Should Be Emphasized in Physical Education Activities* (2:1). As much as possible, teachers should refrain from endless practice sessions solely for the purposes of presenting programs or demonstrations. Administrators and teachers should remember that physical education activities are primarily for the benefit of the *children*. Perfection in activities should not be emphasized until the pupils themselves indicate such an interest.

If interschool athletics are promoted, this should be done only after this question is answered: Are the *primary* purposes of the program to provide enjoyment and educational opportunities *for the pupils* or is there a less defensible purpose, such as to serve as a "feeder" program for secondary school athletes?

5. *A Physical Fitness Testing Program Should Be Established.* A testing program will be worthwhile only if teachers *use* test results as a means of improvement in those areas in which pupils are found to be deficient. For example, if pupils are found to score low in arm and shoulder strength, activities may be selected to help overcome these weaknesses.

As suggested by the President's Council on Youth Fitness, the following screening tests may be given to identify the underdeveloped pupil: (1) pull-ups—to measure arm and shoulder strength, (2) sit-ups —to measure flexibility and abdominal strength, and (3) squat thrusts —to measure agility (5:19). Minimum passing scores and testing procedures are described by the President's Council on Youth Fitness in the publication entitled *Youth Physical Fitness—Suggested Elements of a School-Centered Program, Parts One and Two.*

The American Association for Health, Physical Education and Recreation has devised a youth fitness test battery for grades five through twelve. In the test battery are included three aquatic tests (for those schools with swimming programs) plus the following physical fitness tests: (1) pull-ups (for boys) or modified pull-ups (for girls), (2) sit-ups, (3) standing broad jump, (4) shuttle run, (5) 50-yard dash, (6) softball throw for distance and (7) 600 yard run-walk (1:5). Percentile tables based on age and also tables using the Neilson-Cozens Classification Index are included in the booklet entitled *AAHPER Youth Fitness Test Manual.*

Other physical fitness tests which may be used in elementary schools are the A.A.U. Junior Physical Fitness Test, California Physical Performance Test, Kraus-Weber Test, Minnesota Physical Efficiency Test, Rogers Physical Fitness Index and the Washington Elementary School Physical Fitness Test (3:48).

In addition to physical fitness tests, numerous tests are available to evaluate motor skills in specific activities.

6. *A School Resource Library in the Field of Physical Education Should Be Established.* This should include outstanding books on elementary school physical education, publications of the national government, state and local physical education guidebooks, publications concerning the construction of physical education equipment and supplies, and magazines dealing with the area of physical education.

7. *Special Teachers of Physical Education Should Be Employed in Those School Systems Which Presently Have None.* Also, it may

be necessary to employ additional special teachers in those systems which currently employ one or more. At this time, it may not be practical for the special teachers to conduct all classes, but they can greatly improve the programs by working closely with classroom teachers.

Cooperation is necessary between school administrators, physical education special teachers, classroom teachers and others who may be involved in the program. To prevent misunderstanding, all persons concerned should be fully informed of the administrative organization.

In colleges and universities, interested students should be given every encouragement to enter the field of elementary school physical education. Duties and employment opportunities should be thoroughly explained to them.

8. *Funds for Necessary Facilities, Equipment and Supplies Should Be Provided.* Funds are necessary for the acquisition of grassy play areas, asphalt or concrete play areas, playground apparatus, pull-up bars, phonographs, records, balls, bats, and other equipment.

9. *Classroom Teachers Should Attempt to Improve Themselves Professionally in Physical Education.* This may be accomplished by reviewing publications in elementary school physical education; taking additional courses in physical education; attending conferences and workshops; participating in in-service education; working closely with physical education special teachers; and consulting with superior elementary school teachers, outstanding secondary school physical education instructors and other qualified persons.

Better physically-educated boys and girls will naturally result and better prepared youngsters will be entering the secondary schools.

BIBLIOGRAPHY

1. *AAHPER Youth Fitness Test Manual.* Washington, D.C., American Association for Health, Physical Education and Recreation. 1961. pp. 5.
2. Hein, Fred V., "Not Just Exercise." American Medical Association. December, 1957. pp. 1-2.
3. Miller, Arthur G. and Virginia Whitcomb. *Physical Education in the Elementary School Curriculum.* Englewood Cliffs, N.J.: Prentice-Hall, Inc., 1963. pp. 48-51.
4. Neilson, N. P. and Winifred Van Hagen. *Physical Education for Elementary Schools.* New York: A. S. Barnes and Company. 1954. pp. 39.
5. President's Council on Youth Fitness. *Youth Physical Fitness: Suggested Elements of a School-Centered Program, Parts One and Two.* Washington, D.C.: U.S. Government Printing Office. 1961. pp. 19.

Elementary School Physical Education
MARGARET MILLER

We learn through the study of child growth and development that the years a child spends in elementary school, particularly his early years, are ones in which basic attitudes, behaviour and movement patterns are formed which may endure throughout life. As both a parent and a physical educator, I am concerned about the quality of the physical education experience my child is having in her elementary school, and I am concerned because I know her experience is not unique. The things I would want for my child in physical education at this level, and the things I want for all children as a physical educator are basically the same. These things seem important to me:

1. I want her to have an opportunity to participate in a variety of vigorous physical activities since both her need and her capacity for activity seem limitless.
2. I want her to *enjoy* participating and to develop the desire to be a participant in activity rather than an observer.
3. I want her to be challenged by what she is taught at each level of her school; but basically, I want her *to be taught.*
4. I want her to understand that sports and physical activities are equally as important a part of life for girls as they are for boys.
5. I want her to reap the social and psychological benefits which accrue from participation in group games and activities.
6. I want her teacher to feel that physical education is important because my daughter understands that what is important to the teacher is important to her; and what the teacher doesn't bother with doesn't matter very much.

I am concerned because, through observation, I see few of these things happening to her, and realize that these things happen in very few elementary schools. I see her standing in line for a turn on the bars which may come once during the period. During her physical education period, I see her class stand squirming as the teacher tries to keep them still long enough for everyone to take his turn individually at a skill. I see a teacher who lacks the "know how" to handle her class on the playground. I watch the natural play of children during their recess periods and see that much of it consists of running and jumping and racing and competing with one another ... yet the teacher fails to use or channel these natural desires for vigorous activity. And then I realize that the basic concern of the elementary teacher is only with rather formal social and group learnings which accompany sports and games and *not* with the physical or developmental values. Not that these are not important to me also, but it is obvious that her interest in developing physical skill is very limited.

The Kraus-Weber, as well as the AAHPER tests have shown us that our American children fall below the standards of European children physically. My personal experiences in teaching physical education in an English comprehensive school have shown me conclusively that English children *are* far ahead of their American counterparts in terms of strength, flexibility and endurance. In attempting to analyze the differences in the experiences of the English children and of our children which may account for such marked differences, I find the following things based purely on personal observation:

1. English children participate in gymnastic types of activities, those requiring both strength and flexibility from a very early age. I remember from my own childhood in England, that I dressed for physical training and participated in balancing, tumbling, jumping and rope climbing at six or seven years of age. (They had elementary school physical education specialists in England in the 1930's!) With a movement and activity background like this, teachers of older children have much to build upon.

2. The athletic or sports minded girl is "in" in England. Competition to make school teams is keen, and rivalry between schools is high. Competition has never been *bad,* but has always been a natural and desirable part of sports. Women and girls, as well as men and boys are seen actively participating in leisure time sporting events. The national love of sports and *involvement in sports* must be reflected in the games programs in the elementary schools, and in teacher and community attitude toward the value of sports.

3. The English feeling about sportsmanship and playing the game is well known, but one seldom hears it discussed in relation to school sports programs. This is understood. The important thing is learning to play the game for the sake of the game itself, for the enjoyment of the activity itself. In this country, particularly in the early years, I feel that the social learnings have become more important than the activity. We attempt to teach sportsmanship but not sport.

4. English families seem more conscious of the importance of physical activity. One often sees families out for a walk in the evening or on a Sunday afternoon. They are seen bicycling together. Walking tours and Sunday hikes are common among groups of young people. These attitudes toward activity must be observed and absorbed by children.

With these points in mind, I have been wondering what we are doing, or can do, to bring about desired changes for elementary children. The most obvious step is that of positive teacher training in physical education, or the employment of physical education specialists. But where this is not possible, there are several other things to consider:

1. *Parent or family concern:* The Physical Education supervisor in one system of elementary schools has initiated a series of parent education pamphlets exploring the values of various types of activities (running, jumping, walking) and asking parents to encourage their children to participate during their play hours at home. These are made attractive by self-testing devices. I believe this idea has great possibilities.

2. *A more aggressive elementary school program:* Since we express so much concern over this problem, I have often wondered why qualified physical education personnel, particularly those in teacher education institutions, don't organize themselves in such a way that they are available for in-service programs for teachers or as consultants to school districts which lack P.E. personnel. Our aggressive interest as a profession could help to spark some enthusiasm.

   The new Girl Scout program is organized around a series of challenges which girls must meet at different points in the program. Perhaps such a series of challenges, based on physical skills, could be devised for use in elementary schools and planned in such a way that they could be carried out by classroom teachers. Wherever we can, in those schools where there are qualified personnel, we should encourage the teaching of beginning gymnastics skills, particularly those requiring strength and flexibility and the use of the arms and shoulder girdle.

3. *Additional interest in sports for women and girls:* The new trend toward interscholastic competition for high school girls may help to reawaken the interest of more of them to participate. Some of this enthusiasm, it is hoped, may be transmitted to younger girls and eventually to their children.

Have you evaluated the program in YOUR school recently? What changes, additions, or improvements are needed?

Individualized Physical Activity
JEAN M. YOUNG

"Norman! Get down from that tree." "Norman! Don't climb that fence." "Norman! Look out for those cars!" Norman's outdoors is a small, fenced yard. Lack of room and his mother's fears restrict him from doing all the running, jumping, and climbing he wants and needs to do, but he is more fortunate than many children. He does have a yard and a tree. Norman and all children need to find opportunities for the physical activity which serves as a base for all phases of growth and development, but such opportunities are not easily come by in the environment in which they live.

A child who lives in an apartment cannot run and jump and climb indoors. Even if he had room enough, these activities would be too noisy. He cannot go outside to play because of dangerous traffic. Instead of running and jumping and climbing, he sits and watches television.

A child learns about himself and the world around him in many ways, but most of all by doing—by smelling, hearing, seeing, feeling, running, jumping, stretching, and turning.

Play activities help a child form concepts. Often terms like *inside, outside, on top of, flat, round, wide, big, and far,* acquire their first meanings for him as he plays. In play he learns directions, distance, and force. He learns about gravity through discovering what his body can do in relation to it—how far he can lean without falling, and how he can balance on different parts of his body. He recognizes speed and force as a thrown ball comes toward him, and he learns what he must do in response to speed and force in order to catch the ball.

When a child has limited opportunities to participate in activities such as those described above, his further learning, his total growth, is restricted.

For this reason, the physical education program at the primary level in the Pontiac, Michigan, school system seeks to focus on activity-oriented skills which will enhance the total growth and development of each child. It is a program of sensory-motor activities geared to meet individual needs.

Children are questioned: "How many ways can you bend?" "Why do some parts of your body bend and others not?" They are directed: "Bend a little." "Bend a lot." "Bend something on the upper part of your body." "Bend to the right." "Bend ... and think in which sport you would bend like that."

Motor skills and concepts such as those of direction and force are developed through directed activities: "Find a big ball and practice bouncing it." "How many ways can you bounce the ball?" "Bounce the ball high ... low." "How low can you bounce the ball and still keep it bouncing?" "Can you move around the ball and keep it bouncing?" "Can you move backward ... sideward with the ball and keep it bouncing?" "Can you move with the ball while everyone else is moving and not touch anyone?" "Can you control the ball with your feet by following a line on the floor?"

The activities become more challenging. "What actions can you do while bouncing the ball?" "Put two actions together ... four actions together." "Work out a way of joining the actions to make a smooth pattern." "Can you bounce the ball to someone else while he is bouncing his ball to you?" "How far can you throw the ball and still catch it before it hits the floor?"

Other activities may include imitative movements, work with mats and tether balls, exploration with cardboard boxes, and use of obstacle courses and gymnastic apparatus.

Sensory-motor programs have diagnostic value. In such programs teachers look for tenseness, hyper-activity, explosive movements, inability to concentrate and to solve problems, and lack of established patterns of movement in their pupils.

Screening devices are used in helping to determine the need for medical referrals.

The success of sensory-motor programs in the Pontiac schools has led to several developments:

In Project Head Start, a physical education teacher was assigned to a specific phase of the program to teach the children, to provide equipment, and to work with teachers, parents, and student aides.

A Manual of Motor-Perceptual Activities has been prepared to familiarize physical education teachers and classroom teachers with problem-solving, diagnostic, and activity-oriented programs.

In-service education opportunities are available for teachers who show capabilities and interest in sensory-motor programs. Educational activities include visiting nearby communities which also have sensory-motor programs, observing and teaching with experienced teachers within the system, attending workshops, and taking observation trips to perceptual development centers and universities.

A two-year pilot program was inaugurated in September, in which selected schools place increased emphasis on a physical education program in the primary grades rather than in the traditional upper elementary grade program. The program calls for demonstrations, consultations, classroom teacher directives, testing, and parent follow-up.

This program, by emphasizing physical activities from minimal levels to optimum challenges for each child, must by its intent be individualized. When programs are individualized, many forces focus on the child, and it is here that the educational team—classroom teachers and specialists together—realize a higher potential in the teaching-learning process because they are a team working for the greatest benefit for each child.

Physical Education
in the Elementary School
PAUL SMITH

Physical education is primarily concerned with the physical manipulation of the most perfectly developed, complex and interesting of known organisms—the human body. Marvels of this body have been copied by engineers for centuries in the construction of buildings, bridges and machines. The complexity and infinite potential of this human machine can be immensely frightening to teachers.

Elementary teachers confronted with 35 squirming children may shy at their responsibility for teaching a subject involving physical skill. Unfortunately, most elementary teachers have had very few physical education experiences in their professional preparation. Contemplating their plight, they are faced with the realization that, to teach physical education, a background of physical skills plus a knowledge of the whys and hows of teaching these skills is essential. Since accidents are invited by the unskilled and since skirts and nylons are not conducive to vigorous activity, many elementary teachers tend to shun the instructional aspects of physical education. Therefore, the teaching of skills is spotty. Experience indicates again and again that example is the best teacher, and the teacher may be the only book some of the students ever read. Frightened, ill prepared, poorly coordinated and inappropriately dressed, the classroom teacher is presented a frustrating task, conducive to criticism and failure.

Ideally, specialists in each building could solve most of the elementary physical education problems. Since this is a moot question at present, conscientious classroom teachers must find resources at their disposal to assist them in their preparation for physical education. City, district, county or state coordinators of physical education have a wealth of teaching materials including grade level guides, card files, films, books, records and lists of other resource people. Coordinators should also be available to conduct periodic in-service classes or workshops.

Educational television will provide limited to almost endless opportunities as its potential is explored: limited in remote areas; almost endless in urban areas. Through television, districts can provide a specialist in the classroom. In the meantime, the classroom teacher is responsible for providing the basics of movement to his students. Swimming probably provides the ideal example of what is basic—for every swimming instructor soon discovers that until a child learns to relax and permit the unseen forces of the water to support him, there is little likelihood of his learning to swim. The supporting forces that tend to buoy the child toward efficient basic sports movement are good posture, running, jumping, climbing, balancing, and throwing, catching, bouncing, shooting, kicking and batting a ball. Simple games and relays employing the use of the basic movements, plus daily fitness activities, will provide a firm foundation upon which all movement skills may build.

Movement Education

Movement is an inherent characteristic of the human being. Efficient movement, however, must be learned and developed through directed experience, supervised experimentation, imitation, or by pure accident. Movement education, in the past, has generally been associated with so-called modern dance. Indeed, modern dance experts have provided leadership and have imparted impetus to movement education. Changes, however, are in the making. Any type of movement, whether it be postural correction, leaping through the air, sports skills, work or play, will soon be considered movement education by informed educators.

More activity for all children is a trend today in elementary physical education. The cat chasing the rat around a circle of inactive boys and girls is no longer symbolic of an activity program. Emphasis is on physical fitness skills in which all children can participate at once during much of the activity period.

Teachers will find improvising an interesting and stimulating activity for all. For example, animal walks are known to be excellent total body developers; therefore, it may be advisable to substitute certain selected animal walks for standing in various games and relays. Taking a crab walk position in such simple games as keep away, hot ball, and dodge ball (in which the ball is pushed with one foot) is not only stimulating to children but also a vigorous physical conditioner. Standing, running and dodging in the face up, all fours, crab walk position tend to draw the shoulders back and strengthen the arms, legs and stomach, in addition to developing endurance.

Imaginative responses to, "How many ways can you hop, jump or leap?" will provide subject matter for several active sessions. Application of the jumping or hopping idea to animals might suggest kangaroos, frogs, rabbits, grasshoppers, bucking horses or crickets. Suggestions of jumping or hopping toys might result in jacks-in-the-box, rope skipping bears, pogo sticks, or Mexican jumping beans.

Interpreting a day at the circus, farm, zoo or pet shop, where primary children demonstrate the animals visited, will generate enthusiastic activity for days. More elaborate performances for assemblies or parents might include simple headpieces made of colored art paper and stapled together to form animal likenesses.

Shadow Practice

Equipment and supplies are desirable and generally necessary for the most effective physical education classes, but creative teachers with imagination will find ways of circumventing almost any obstacle. All skills for games involving equipment may be taught and practiced without the equipment, especially in the preliminary stages of learning. Throwing, catching, bowling, passing, dribbling, shooting, batting and stroking a ball may be taught without ball or bat. Finesse of the movement is the objective. The rhythmic pattern of the skill soon becomes so ingrained with practice that when equipment is used, undivided attention is devoted to timing and accuracy.

Pugilists have for generations used shadow boxing as a conditioner and means of sharpening the timing for intricate boxing moves. Shadow practice in other sports skills will permit all children in a class to practice at once by pantomiming or pretending to do the skill. No equipment is necessary during shadow practice, but a record player is recommended to set the tempo for the movement. Sixty one-hand basketball setshots may be executed by a fourth grade class in one minute using the shadow method of instruction. By means of comparison, in a class of 30 children, with four basketballs to the class, it would take more than two hours for each child to have the same number of practice shots at a goal. As the number of children in the class is increased or the quantity of balls is decreased, the difference becomes greater. Making a goal while performing under the severe scrutiny of one's peers often makes early practice with a ball tense, unnatural movement. Shadow practice will eliminate these pressures and may be used to teach or review many elements of movement skills from rope skipping to soccer dribbling whether or not equipment is readily accessible. It is true that if ball skills are taught using the shadow method, balls must be used eventually or interest will wane.

Study of mechanical equipment on a field trip, or through pictures, followed by interpretations of their movement, helps primary children sharpen their techniques of observation, plus increasing the flexibility of their bodies. Equipment may be classified according to use such as: construction (bulldozer, crane, ditch digger, loader, dump truck, pile driver, earth mover and tamper); transportation (piston engine, automobile, airplane, motor boat and draw bridge); miscellaneous (washing machine, oil well pump, farm equipment and others). After imitating individual pieces of machinery, teachers may suggest that children work in complementary groups: a bulldozer piles the dirt; a loader lifts it into the dump truck; the truck hauls the load to a dump.

Meeting Equipment Needs

Originality in use of available school furniture and cast-off equipment challenges teachers and students to do the most with what they have. Tables and benches can become tunnels and vaulting boxes. Two chairs are converted into a set of parallel bars for the execution of simple stunts. A mop handle is transformed into a ball bat, golf club, wand, roller or crank for swinging, jumping, pushing, pulling or twisting. Jump ropes turn into dancing partners, discarded bowling pins pass as dumbbells, bicycle inner tubes are used as stretching devices, and surplus ropes and cargo nets are made into climbers. All of these substitute equipment innovations are adaptable to most ages and grade levels, but the skills involved in each should have a planned progression through the grades like all other development skills.

Currently literature by optometrists, psychologists, and remedial reading specialists reinforces convictions of physical educators that there is a direct relationship between bilateral movement skills and academic achievement in most young children. It has generally been accepted that increased circulation of the blood to the brain, caused by exercise, makes the individual more alert and better prepared to meet mental problems and stresses. Future curricula should provide primary teachers with a sequential series of exercises to develop bilateral movement skills of children, which in turn will reinforce their reading and writing skills. Included should be: animal walks in all fours positions; balance beam skills; ball rolling, tossing, catching, bouncing and dribbling; and coordination skills. These, with other related activities, will be suggested as a means of increasing a child's academic potential.

Before a child is able to sit for reasonably long periods of time reading and writing, words and/or numbers, normal sequacious physical development must have preceded. Muscles control the eyes in reading, the hands and fingers in writing, and the trunk in the sitting posture. These muscles need to be conditioned for their function in reading and writing (witness the restlessness of the primary child after a half hour of seatwork). Muscles controlling the eyes and fingers are small. Small muscles develop more slowly than the large arm, leg and trunk muscles. The infant uses his large muscles almost immediately in sweeping movements of the arms and legs. Continued development finds him turning himself over, crawling, pulling himself up to his feet and finally walking. Knowledge of his surroundings is enhanced by his ability to move freely about to explore his environment. But suddenly, the child is placed in a classroom setting where large movements disturb others. A transition period is necessary in order for children to change from active home life to the semi-active classroom.

Each boy or girl has but one life. How he spends his time at work or play depends largely on how teachers have influenced and prepared him. A healthy, physically fit child has the capacity to face the world. Interaction of mind and body is most apparent to the observant teacher. A sick child is unable to concentrate or move efficiently. Poor posture might mirror insecurity, uneasiness, timidity or self-consciousness. Self-confidence, alertness and forcefulness are generally reflected in good posture. The insecure child is unable to perform to his physical or mental potential and, conversely, the child may become more insecure by his inability to perform physically or mentally. Tensions and anxieties are released through sports and games so that a child's entire outlook may be changed by an improved feeling of well-being. Elementary teachers can be prepared to meet these challenges of the complex child.

The Developmental Approach

THOMAS R. BURKE

Since the developmental process from childhood to adolescence is gradually changing it seems immature to assume that contemporary educational objectives would, therefore, remain consistent. The psychological and physical structure of the modern student is in a stage of evolution—i.e., from a selfish, meaningless, and physically underdeveloped child to a potentially social, purposeful and physically well-developed teenager. In view of these characteristics it seems that the physical education objectives and program content at the elementary level of instruction would not be the same as those objectives and program content at the secondary level of instruction. In preparing a curriculum for grades one through twelve, it is necessary to keep this evolution in mind.

Physical

One of the main purposes of physical education in the elementary schools is for students to learn physical skills necessary for ordinary games and physical activities that are highly valued in childhood—

such skills as throwing and catching, kicking, tumbling, and handling simple tools. Havinghurst states that

> The peer group rewards a child for success and punishes
> him by indifference for failure in this task (3).

This is a period, grades one through eight, of general growth of muscle and bone. Large muscle coordination precedes that of small muscles. The refinements of neuromuscular skill come at the end rather than at the beginning of this period. The more skillful activities would thus be taught prior to the onset of adolescence.

Social

A second objective is for the student to build wholesome attitudes toward himself as a maturing person. Physical growth is taking place, and muscles are developing rapidly. The child is attempting to develop an ability to enjoy and care for his body. Many children are approved or disapproved by their peers because of their physique and physical skills.

This awareness of the self is culturally based. There is a considerable stress on appearance and physical performance in American culture (3). The body is regarded as a source of pleasure and of value. Children are constantly discovering new ways to express themselves physically. This high value can be interpreted as an end result of successful performance in which the experience of success was intrinsic to the student. Exploratory movements, both rhythmic and non-rhythmic are a source of pleasure. Active games are also greatly enjoyed in this age period.

Socially, the youngster at the elementary level is encouraged to get along with his peers. Through physical activity the youngster learns the give and take of social life among his age mates. He learns to make friends and to get along with enemies, "He develops a social personality" (4). The child learns ways of approaching strangers. He learns what it means to "play fair" in games. Once he has learned these social habits, he often tends to continue them throughout life. The physical education class is one of the main places where children learn to get along with their age mates.

> Whether the teacher pays any attention to it or not, the
> child's chief concern is with this task (3).

The student is learning to be a boy or a girl—to act the role that is expected and rewarded. In the early grades, girls bodies are as well formed for physical activities as are boys bodies. It is not until high school that the anatomical differences become quite apparent. Earlier the girls outperform the boys on many occasions.

Program

The core of program for grades one through eight is movement. The basic movements of walking, jumping, hopping, running, leaping, bending, stretching, pushing, pulling, turning, shaking, and bouncing are the foundations from which other movements are derived. In the early grades, the emphasis is in developing skill, using these movements in an atmosphere which focuses on the child as a developing individual. In later elementary grades, the more organized forms of activity—games, sports, stunts, tumbling, rhythms, and dance—are then built on combinations of these basic movements.

Areas of Concentration

From grades one through six there are three regions of activity concentration. *The first* is made up of fundamental skills and games of low organization. The fundamental skills, mentioned previously, are directed specifically toward the objectives of skill development and the awareness of self. The majority of educators suggest that most children of this group see the need for developing skill and control. Jersild and Havighurst, for example, believe that skill development in the physical education class is a key formulator of the "self concept" (1). (See page 88, Table I)

Games of low organization, although vigorous in nature, are directed toward the socialization objective. Group games, individual and dual games, help to satisfy the individual desire to belong to, and be liked by the group.

> Most eight- and nine-year-olds would rather be with the group than be alone. Group games offer an effective way of further developing some of the qualities essential for sound inter-personal relationships (3,4).

The awareness of the self as a growing organism is best accomplished through activities which are exploratory and seeking in context.

The second area at the early elementary level is focused on this prospective. These gymnastic type activities would include stunts, exercise, apparatus work, and individual self-testing activities. The method of instruction is based on the Schopenhauer notion which allows the child to arrive at his desired movement naturally (8). In other words, a model of a movement is not presented to the child. The move that the child develops through his own trial and error is the model that the child adapts. In grades one through six all activities would be taught in this manner. For this reason classification procedures and ability grouping mechanisms would not be valid.

The *third area of concentration* within grades one through six is rhythmics. Developing skill in locomotor movements is important to boys and girls. They like to walk, hop, and jump to the accompaniment of the piano, phonograph, tom-tom, etc. Boys and girls enjoy the non-locomotor movements like bending and stretching.

Children like to experiment with changes of tempo, direction, accent, and level (2).

Children learn varied movement skills to these auditory cues. They learn to appreciate themselves as a moving organism.

Upper Elementary

In grades seven and eight *the shift is to activities that require greater skill,* but some of the earlier grade programs are retained with less emphasis. Skill in team games such as football, basketball, and volleyball is desirable for this group. Interest in these activities is high. Team games are an important part of the curriculum at this age because they give boys and girls experience in planning and working together on problems that seem important to them and at the same time improve human relationships. Individual and dual type of sports are now introduced. Previously, tennis and badminton were not recommended activities because neuromuscular coordination and muscular development was still too low.

The rhythmic and gymnastic activities are retained, but with less amplification. The focus for twelve and thirteen year old students is a continued refinement and coordination of the basic movements. For instance, kicking a football, is dependent upon three basic movements —swinging, bending, and pushing—in relation to such external factors as size and weight of ball, direction, speed, and target. On the other hand, the rhythmical movements are now combined into dance forms, namely folk dances. The further development of social skills with the opposite sex, and the identification of the sex role is uppermost as an important objective throughout such activities as coed folk and square dance.

Secondary School

As the student reaches late adolescence he is now confronted with what he should do when he gets out into the world. He must select and prepare for a profession or an occupation. He begins to develop attitudes toward family life and the role which he will play in society. Because American society is free, the wise use of adult leisure time is a foremost objective. Physical education can contribute to the enhancement of a productive and psychologically wholesome adult life through skill development in activities that are of "adult nature" (3).

These activities—i.e., swimming, tennis, golf, and physical fitness—are valued for their physical and psychological potential contribution to the self "image." (See page 88, Table I)

These *"adult valued activities"* are not taught from a purely technical viewpoint. It is necessary to point out to the student the concomitant attributes of engaging in archery or badminton. For instance, this would bring up questions of the potential social, psychological, and fitness significance at various age levels through adulthood. Not only is skill promoted, but it is hoped that the student will be "liberally educated" in the carry-over activities. A liberal physical education means that the student will be able to select and prepare his own activities based on a reasonable degree of experimental background in many carry-over sports.

Achieving new and more mature relations with age mates of both sexes is based on the premise that

> One of the constant challenges of democracy is to promote the general welfare by directing our interests of the group while encouraging the optimum development of each individual (6).

From age thirteen, most boys and girls are preoccupied with social activities and social experimentation. "This is their most important business" (3). With their own sex they learn to behave as adults among adults, to organize their own athletic activities, to choose leaders. With the opposite sex they learn adult social skills, how to converse, to dance, and to play social games. It is necessary, therefore, to select activities that contribute to leadership, and social behavior with the sexes.

The *final objective* of physical education at the high school level, ages thirteen to eighteen, is to develop within the student an acceptance of his own physique and to use it as effectively as possible. This is a period, physiologically, of great variability in the growth cycle. Psychologically, the attitudes and interests are in a state of change. For instance, slowness of development may be a cause for individual concern. The student should be made aware that this particular problem is normal in the growth cycle. The goal is to help the student to become proud of, or at least tolerant of, the capabilities of his body.

Grouping

It would, therefore, seem appropriate to *group students on the basis of skill development.* Motor skill and fitness classification would help students with similar backgrounds to compete with greater

TABLE I.   A TENTATIVE PROGRAM

MAJOR CONTENT CONCENTRATION	TYPES OF ACTIVITIES	GRADE LEVEL	TEACHING EMPHASIS	SOCIALIZATION	CLASSIFICATION
1. Movement Education	gymnastics, stunts apparatus, self-testing	1 - 6	Child self-discovery	Both sexes are instructed together as one group	None
2. Games of low organization	lead up games to major and minor sports	1 - 6			
3. Rhythms	group and individual exploration to music	1 - 6			
1. Movement Education	combinations of basic movements	7 - 8	Child self-discovery	Separate boys and girls classes, coed for dance, badminton, etc.	None
2. Team games	football, soccer, softball, etc.	7 - 8			
3. Individual and dual sports	tennis, badminton, track	7 - 8			
4. Rhythms	folk dance - coed	7 - 8			
1. Team games	basketball, volleyball, touch football, etc.	9 - 12	Group living Leadership	Separate boys and girls classes, coed for dance, tennis, etc.	Ability grouping
2. Carryover sports	tennis, golf, swimming, individual fitness	9 - 12	Liberalization		
3. Movement Education	gymnastics stunts-apparatus	9 - 12	Self-discovery		
4. Rhythms	social-square round-dance	9 - 12	Socialization between sexes		

satisfaction without the stigma of being picked last and ridiculed for ineptness during game play. The identification of the physically underdeveloped, average, and above average student helps the instructor to specify his instructional goals.

The common heterogenous type of class organization is responsible for much of the physical educators' inability to significantly affect mass developmental techniques which reach the great majority of students (5).

The *program content* is divided into four areas: team sports, carry–over sports, movement education, and rhythms. Aquatics is advisable, but the fact remains that the majority of high schools do not have swimming pools. To solve this problem, arrangements should be made with YMCA's and Boy's Clubs, so students may enroll in aquatics and related activities not being offered at the high school. (See page 88, Table I)

The justification of *team sports* is based on immediacy, response, and socialization principles. Students engage in those activities that are popular within their immediate environment both in and out of school.

The prime educational function of group competitive activity is the promotion of cooperative types of responses and the proper modification of competitive responses, so that both may contribute ultimately to individual and group behavior (6).

Socially, concomitant learnings such as leadership, ability to get along with fellow students, although objectively immeasurable, are qualities that have a good chance of development within a team-like atmosphere.

Carry-over sports such as individual fitness, golf, and tennis are examples of activities to be taught at the high school level. They are called "carry-over sports" because the student can participate in them during adult years. However, it is a mistake to assume that these leisure activities are to be used only by the individual when he becomes an adult. Students also have their leisure time. The goal is for the individual to engage in pursuits of his choosing—a liberal education through physical activity.

Movement education and gymnastics are related activities. Throughout such activities as stunts, tumbling, apparatus work, individual movement through exploration (Mosston method), it is hoped that the student will develop a greater awareness of himself. One goal is to help the student to become proud of his own capabilities. Another goal is the possible improvement in neuromuscular skill, strength, cardiovascular endurance, and flexibility. These activities are conducted within the spirit of self-exploration and discovery.

To develop proper relationships between sexes is partially accomplished through *dance and coed activities*. Girls do not learn the roles related to the social aspects of dance by dancing with other girls. Nor, do boys learn the masculine role within a mixed group through such substitute experiences as the television and the movies. The activities selected are adopted equally as well to the capabilities of both sexes.

Concluding Statement

Thus, it is necessary to examine the curriculum from several viewpoints. The physiological, psychological, and social aspects which are in a state of change during the developing years must be considered. With these points in mind, the curriculum content at the various grade levels would be different.

BIBLIOGRAPHY

1. Andrews, Gladys, et. al *Physical Education for Today's Boys and Girls.* Boston: Allyn and Bacon, 1960.
2. Halsey, Elizabeth. *Inquiry and Invention in Physical Education.* Philadelphia: Lea and Febiger, 1964.
3. Havighurst, Robert J. *Developmental Tasks and Education.* New York: Longmans, Green and Co., 1952.
4. Jersild, Arthur T. *In Search of Self.* New York: Teachers College Press, 1952.
5. LeProtti, Stan. *LaSierra High School Boy's Physical Education Program.*
6. Nixon, John E. and Frederickson, Florence S. *An Introduction to Physical Education.* Philadelphia: W. B. Saunders Co., 1964.
7. Nixon, John E. and Jewett, Ann E. *The Physical Education Curriculum.* New York: Ronald Press Co., 1964.
8. Schopenhaurer, Arthur. "On Education." *Gateway to Great Books,* 1963.

21

A New Look at Elementary School Physical Education

FRANCIS HARMS

American Education today offers many challenges in many fields. We are moving ahead with great strides, just as our society itself calls for. Much of our progress is the result of dedicated teachers who search for new methods of presentation, or who in fact create programs which move us forward in a day when we must be moving. Such is the case in our physical education departments. In this article we shall be taking a new look at Elementary Physical Education and the particular challenge it presented to our school system.

Today we are constantly aware of the need for physical fitness. Much is being done to encourage our citizens to develop their bodies, because our modern world no longer gives us the opportunities it did before automation. The problem, it seems, is to find ways to present material in a way that will have lasting value along with high interest. It is our belief that the program we have developed in the Columbus, Nebraska Elementary Schools answers to a high degree the challenge in this field.

All across this wonderful country of ours, we still find many schools who have done little to advance this part of their students' education. This is true especially in the elementary field. Gone are the days when children came to school fresh from a long walk or a morning's chores completed.

Teachers in the classroom find that students who are in good physical condition also tend to be more mentally alert. Today, we still have many schools who have only a recess period to meet this pressing challenge. Perhaps there was a day when the recess met its needs —but does it today? Let's look at some of the points it seems to lack. When children are free as a group, they tend to play together in small peer groups. Those who for some reason or other are not liked by some are excluded from many activities. In many cases these are the children who may be physically behind and need the activity most. This is also true of many unfortunate boys and girls who have had crippling diseases or brain damage.

We find, too, that it lacks a well rounded program. Favorite games are played day after day, with very little variety. Then the problem of instruction in correct methods, rules, sportsmanship, etc., are often lacking. We have a choice in this area and this author would like to present a program which is working excellently in this city's public elementary schools.

The Plan

In our elementary grades, each first, second and third has a 20 minute physical education period each day. The first 5 minutes are set aside for calisthenics, followed by 15 minutes for the scheduled activity. The fourth, fifth and sixth grades have a 30 minute class each day with 10 minutes for calisthenics. We feel that this continued work on muscle development has paid tremendous dividends. For instance—the test we give our students in the 5th and 6th grades is much like other national tests. It includes squat thrusts, push-ups, pull-ups, sit-ups and jump reach. Those doing all that can be expected at their age level receive a classification of 1, which is excellent, followed by a 2, 3, 4, or a 5. Those getting a 5 are in poor physical condition. These figures represent the average classification of the five part test. In September, 1965, nearly 400 of our 5th and 6th grade students were given this P.E. test. The results are listed below, along with the surprising results of the same test the following months of May and September.

Classification	1	2	3	4	5
Sept. 65	2	44	165	137	50
May 66	31	142	124	77	15
Sept. 66	22	155	136	60	12

During the test given in September, 1966, there was a tremendous increase in the performance over the previous September. This would indicate the carry-over value of such a program. Our tests are administered by the elementary teachers, with help from the Supervisor. Great pains are taken to see that these tests are administered and recorded in a careful and exacting manner in each school. Thus, we feel that these statistics reflect a very worthwhile positive move forward.

The remainder of this program is somewhat unique. Over the years we have experimented and improved upon the type of scheduling until we now feel we have a rather complete and exciting program to offer. Within the school calendar, our students progress from basic steps to the more advanced in quite a number of areas. Some of the activities are softball, touch football, volleyball, newcomb, basketball, track, soccer, indoor and outdoor games, rhythmics, rope jumping, relays, apparatus work, self-testing, scooter cart races, stunts, tumbling and isometrics. The scooter carts work the muscles and develop coordination similar to swimming.

All of the preceding activities are scheduled in season, on a monthly chart resembling a calendar. Thus, the students are engaged in an attractive schedule which never repeats itself within the week. At the school year's end, all areas have had nearly equal time devoted to each. This type of program results in all students being schooled in proper techniques, development of interests and skills in many areas, improved coordination, increased self-confidence as they advance, and great possibilities of carry-over value for their future years.

We use quite a complete series of records in our rhythmic program. They include folk dances and square dances for all of the grades. Thus, these children learn the many steps associated with this type of activity, plus gaining much personal confidence and social benefits. Since all of our classes are co-educational, it provides children with an opportunity to have fun together while learning skills and developing an interest that will pay dividends for years. This is also true in other areas where students learn the fundamentals of many games which will provide them with added spectator interest and social competence.

To make a particular point of this, we might cite just a couple of situations where this type of program can really carry some weight. Students who are taught procedure, fundamentals, rules, and particular formations and plays, and then actual participation during their elementary years, go into the secondary schools in a position to be active participants and interested spectators because of their knowledge of the games. This will carry over in their adult years and, we hope, give them a wider scope of interests with which to enjoy a fuller life. We can be quite sure that the first reason given for non-participation is that of ignorance of the particular activity. Thus, we can see the importance of giving our young people the opportunity to progress in a wide spectrum of activities and even feel the desire to excel in one or more specific areas.

Some Problems

What are the problems that present themselves while initiating such a program in the lower grades? Perhaps the most difficult is orientating the elementary teachers on the need for such a program, and then finding the proper person to supervise the entire program. This is necessary for continuity and uniformity. In our system where we have eight schools throughout the city, the supervisor travels to each school once a week. He spends 1/2 day at each school, personally teaching each class one period per week. Thus, the supervisor helps the teachers by giving instruction on proper techniques and explanation of activities foreign to the classroom teacher. After the program has been underway for a year or so, it naturally smoothes out and this presents an opportunity for even further exploration. Since many schools operate on a much smaller plane, this post may not even be a possibility. This, however, should not hinder a school in setting up a similar type of program.

The cost can vary according to the curriculum. However, it is not necessary to spend great sums. This should not be a big factor, as much of the equipment may already be on hand or is not an expensive item. Another problem is finding the room to use during those periods when the schedule or weather calls for indoor activities. This again is usually not a sufficient reason to stall progress. We are forced in several of our older buildings to use a room that is much too small. It does limit us here somewhat in these schools, but by no means does it impede the overall progress.

Final Statement

We are very proud of our Elementary Physical Education Program. Its success came about because of the efforts of our Board of Education, Physical Education Coordinator and Supervisor, and most important, the positive attitude of our teachers. We hope many other schools will soon begin taking action in this field. Where else can you find the natural interests and biological drives so prevalent as in these eager boys and girls? It's just another step in the education of the total human being.

Creativity in Physical Education

BILLY JEAN LITTLE

"Let your imagination soar, then engineer it down to earth." ...

Giving students the opportunity to explore, investigate, express, experience and reorganize is an experience which should be afforded in the physical education class as well as in the art lab, the dance studio or the drama class. It is the outstanding teacher who uses all of his imaginative and inventive powers to allow time for creative performance during the physical education class period. It shall be the purpose of this article to describe various opportunities for the physical educator to foster creativity in his students, and the opportunities he has to be creative in his own teaching.

Developing Creativity

Opportunities are many for introducing the student to exercises in creative exploration in the physical education class.

Establishing the climate or atmosphere for creativity is very important, as there should be several ingredients present in order to offer a greater opportunity for the student to become creatively involved. When allowing students to create a new game, a new exercise, fencing, tumbling or swimming routine, the physical educator should allow adequate time for both practice and demonstration. Students should be encouraged to toy with ideas of their own choosing with provision of time when they can be free to explore, and then perform.

Sincere complimentary evaluation of student action is necessary when encouraging creative performance. Students should be free to try things out and should never be restricted in their creative involvement to the point where they are afraid they are performing incorrectly.

When presenting the student with a problem in creativity, the physical educator should also be sure the problem is specifically understood by the individual or the group involved. Should the problem not be clearly understood and questions therefore arise, the teacher should be careful to redefine the problem, as opposed to giving an answer or suggestion which might interrupt the truly creative process.

Opportunities for creative exploration are at the fingertips of the teacher. Where else but in the gymnasium, on the playing field, the swimming pool or the tennis court may a child become involved with: various balls; a multiple of skills and a variety of activities; a program involving the varied use of equipment and facilities; as well as an ideal situation where mental as well as physical stimulation can be obtained through the various means of competition? Where else but in the physical education class can creativity be possible for both student and teacher due to neither being limited to the truly necessary confines of a class textbook?

Teaching students to see potentialities in all physical things offers the teacher of physical education another opportunity for encouraging creativity on the part of the student. Being able to relate the skills of one sport to that of another, as well as being able to inculcate a desire and an appreciation for creative use of leisure time activity is an opportunity which should not be overlooked by the physical educator.

Activity classes in team sports should be allowed time for reflective thinking for purposes of thinking out strategy and team play. With previously guided and planned learning experiences presented by the teacher, creativity of student-planned strategy will occur easily and successfully.

In the selection of other problems, it might be wise for the physical educator to first study the environment of small children. For when children are allowed to play at will, they can: think of more things to do with a ball; make up new games; and find new uses for traditional pieces of equipment. It is the child who possesses natural physical creative behavior. Would it not be wise to study the play habits of this most creative individual with natural tendencies?

Some Problems

Although numerous in scope, a few selected problems for physical creative involvement might include:

— Creating an exercise routine in time to music, a rhythm beat, or the reading of a poem.

— Creating a new game involving the use of a playground ball or a bean bag.

— Exploration of a movement from a stimulus given by a phrase of music or a verbal description.

— Creating a tumbling routine.
— Creating a new folk dance to the music of an old familiar song.
— Discovering new, free movements on pieces of gym apparatus equipment.
— Exploring the action and use of various balls.
— Letting students experiment with varying rules and restrictions.
— Creating a jump rope routine.
— Creating a swimming routine.

Developing a Creative Physical Educator

Selecting specific characteristics of a creative physical educator involves selecting a teacher who experiments with new methods of teaching skills, techniques of teaching and coaching hints.

It is the creative physical educator who knows when to add another ball to a game which is slowing, present a new rule to a game which is no longer challenging, or change a drill formation into a quick, competitive relay.

A creative teacher is not a memorizer, he is a thinker, a searcher who is constantly experimenting with new approaches to teaching. He is the teacher who makes his subject matter take on life.

If a teacher is attempting to develop creativity in others, he should first develop his own creative consciousness. From there the teacher can then begin to challenge the creative ability of others. To expose creative behavior, the teacher should not be totally concerned about the quality of performance, but should encourage a permissive environment. Actually, it should be the creative teacher who has an inquisitive nature and who probes for the best method of directing the creative talents of his students. He should discover when to leave the student alone during exploration, and when to offer a suggestion which would lend itself toward increasing the student's degree of creativity. The teacher, however, must be ever conscious of over-directing and over-manipulating the student.

Besides having an inquisitive and exploratory nature, the creative teacher should also possess the characteristics of flexibility. If a game calls for ten Indian clubs, but the teacher finds he has none, the creative teacher might attempt to use empty milk cartons. If a game involves only a few players, but there is a need to have all class members active, a flexible and creative teacher would modify the rules to include all students. If a student continually throws his softball bat, the teacher can require the student to carry his bat down to first base with him, or have him complete his swing and lay the bat on a towel lying near to the base.

Bringing creativity into a physical educator's daily routine can also be obtained through the use and choice of meaningful, but colorful words. It is surprising how the use of a fresh, new verbal expression proves to be more stimulating than an old trite expression which is heard time after time. Such an expression as "Kick the ball off the top of the shoelaces," might add more zip to a class than that of, "Kick the ball off the top of the instep." Fluency of speech can greatly characterize the creative teacher.

Concluding Statement

What a challenge it can be to create new teaching devices, new methods, new problems to present to the physical education class! Should thoughts ever cease? No! They should continually tend to become more alive and vibrant for the truly creative teacher!

Are you, as a physical educator encouraging your students to develop and express their own ideas and feelings? It is through physical creative experiences where the individual is allowed to fully use his body as an instrument for expression that this occurs.

It might be said that the human resource most needed in today's world of conformity and confusion is that of creative thinking. Developing creative thinking talents in students is a universal endeavor which should be explored by all disciplines of the education process.

What must be realized is that the field of physical education is a fertile, still undeveloped one. New games, new equipment, new teaching methods and devices are needed, and it will only be the creative educator who will permit his imagination to soar to the heights, and then bring his thoughts and his dreams down to earth, to that which is real.

Seven Guides to Creativity

E. PAUL TORRANCE

I have a tremendous respect for the potential contribution of health education, physical education, and recreation programs to the development of creative thinking abilities and the use of these abilities to acquire knowledge. Educators generally have limited the definition of "knowledge" and "intellectual development" to narrowly linguistic aspects. Because of this and other misconceptions, fields such as health education, physical education, and recreation have been handicapped in coming into their own, insofar as the development of the ability to think creatively is concerned.

For the past seven years, I have been engaged in a program of research in schools and colleges relative to the development of the creative thinking abilities, creative ways of learning, and the conditions that make possible healthy creative growth. These studies have involved children, young people, and adults at all educational levels from kindergarten through graduate school in a variety of localities in the United States and in several countries outside of the United States. The incidents, although few, in which I have specifically studied the development of the creative thinking abilities through health education, physical education, and recreation have convinced me that these fields can make important contributions to the general freeing and development of the creative thinking abilities in schools. I also believe that this program of research has given me some valid insights about the things that can be done to make this contribution.

An Experience in Creative Movement

A key experience that has made me aware of the potential of these fields was my excursion to observe the work in creative movement conducted by Gertrude Baker, former head of the Department of Physical Education for Women at the University of Minnesota, in the primary grades of a local school. As I observed her first and second grade groups, it seemed obvious that they were engaged in a great deal of very sound creative thinking and that development was occurring. I was particularly impressed with their use of the warm-up experience, the fluency of the ideas expressed in movement, the flexibility and originality of thinking manifested, and the way in which they elaborated their ideas. I was immediately curious to know what effect this was having on the development of their creative thinking abilities. Arrangements were then made in February 1964 to administer a battery of the Minnesota Tests of Creative Thinking (Non-Verbal Form B) to the first and second grade classes that had been working with Dr. Baker for about five months and to the third grade class with which she had just started working. The battery included the Picture Construction, Incomplete Figures, and Closed Figures Tests.

Much to our surprise, we found that almost one-half of the first and second graders achieved scores that exceeded the mean for the fifth grade on measures such as fluency, flexibility, originality, and elaboration. Not one of the 42 third graders just beginning the creative movement class achieved a score that reached this level.

The third graders were retested, with an alternate form of the creative thinking test, however, in May after about four months of work in creative movement. As shown on the table on page 102, the growth in fluency, flexibility and originality were dramatic. Only the ability to elaborate failed to show a statistically significant gain.

Perhaps more dramatic than these statistics were some of the changes that occurred in the development of individual children. For example, one third grade boy had created problems in the classroom for some time. His participation in classroom learning activities was minimal and he manifested hostility in many ways. At first he also manifested hostility in the creative movement class. As he found acceptable ways of expressing hostility through movement, his hostility began to diminish and he began to participate in the creative movement class with absorption. Similarly, his general classroom attitude was transformed. His parents also noted a difference.

Suggested Guidelines for Creative Teaching

Drawing now from a variety of studies (Torrance, 1962, 1963, 1965), I shall suggest a few guidelines that will be productive in developing creative thinking abilities through health education, physical education, and recreational programs in schools.

1. DO NOT LEAVE CREATIVE DEVELOPMENT TO CHANCE

Only a few years ago, it was commonly thought that all kinds of creativity had to be left to chance. Similarly, it was believed that gifted performances in physical education and recreational activities had to be left to chance, after practice, drill, and rigorous training regimes had been observed. High level performances have been regarded as artistry and have been clothed with an air of the mysterious. Deliberate methods of creative problem solving were rarely used.

With the demonstrated successes of deliberate methods of problem solving in recent years, it is difficult to understand how a well-informed person can still hold these views. The record of inventions, scientific discoveries, and other creative achievements and evidences of creative growth is impressive.

2. ENCOURAGE CURIOSITY AND OTHER CREATIVE CHARACTERISTICS

Beginning quite early, natural curiosity has been discouraged in children as though it were something unnatural and evil. Whole areas of experiencing and investigation are placed off limits for children because of their sex, social class, race, or religion. This is particularly true in the areas of experience of interest to workers in the fields of health education, physical education, and recreation.

Curiosity about one's own body is especially discouraged; children fail to learn some of the simplest and most fundamental things about their bodily functioning. As a result, they are extremely ineffective in using experiences from their bodies and in developing healthy attitudes concerning the enjoyment of their bodies. Restrictions on this kind of curiosity are more severe on girls than on boys. Numerous studies, for example, indicate that men are more effective than women in using experiences from their bodies and are more aware of and attentive to their bodies.

Using a list of 66 characteristics that have been found to differentiate highly creative people from less creative people, a panel of serious students of the creative personality rated the following ten characteristics as most important in creative functioning (Torrance, 1965):

1. Courage (intellectual courage, courage in convictions)
2. Curiosity
3. Independence in thinking
4. Independence in judgment
5. Willingness to take risks
6. Intuitiveness
7. Absorption in tasks
8. Persistence
9. Unwillingness to accept things on mere say-so
10. Visionary

It should be challenging to design guided, planned learning experiences in health education, physical education, and recreational programs to encourage the development of these and other creative characteristics.

3. BE RESPECTFUL OF QUESTIONS AND UNUSUAL IDEAS

Early in our research, we became convinced that one of the simplest and most powerful ways of encouraging creative growth was to respect the questions that children ask, respect the ideas that they present for consideration, show them that their ideas have value, encourage opportunities for practice and experimentation without evaluation and grading, and encourage and give credit for self-initiated learning and thinking. We made these principles the basis for some of our early teachers' manuals and inservice education programs.

These principles have elicited a wide range of reactions. While some have attacked them as unvalidated hypotheses, others have attacked them as "self-evident truisms and annoyingly pat exhortations." Nevertheless, our observations showed that teachers are generally not very skillful in applying these principles. Even when they try deliberately to do so, some teachers are unable to apply them with any degree of fidelity. Teachers who were able to apply them with fidelity, however, found that their teaching was virtually transformed as a result. Measured changes at a statistically significant level were found in creative growth not found in control groups.

4. RECOGNIZE ORIGINAL, CREATIVE BEHAVIOR

Original, creative behavior is rarely recognized by teachers. One of the things that teachers should work at is to be on the lookout for original, creative solutions among their own students, whether in the classroom, on gymnastic apparatus, or in a basketball game. Most teachers are surprised at the quantity and quality of the sound, original work their students will do.

Almost everyone has been amazed and impressed by the creative achievements of high school students in the summer institutes of the National Science Foundation. New groups of high achievers also emerge when students are taught in such a way that they are permitted to do original thinking and go beyond the mastery of existing knowledge. Jablonski (1964) reports some amazing successes in one of these programs. He believed that if high school students could do such outstanding work in the summer they should continue throughout the school year. Through some of the public schools, he arranged for a continuous program with results that amaze seasoned professional research scientists. He estimates that 25 percent of these high school students are producing publishable research in competition with mature researchers. He then extended this work into the elementary grades and found a readiness for research beyond his expectations. His elementary school group has made some excellent contributions to cancer research projects. One of Jablonski's high school students with an IQ of 86 produced some ideas of his own that some of the "brighter" students are now researching—and that some of the university people are picking up and trying (Jablonski, 1964).

5. ASK QUESTIONS THAT REQUIRE THINKING

Another obvious but not easily achieved thing that almost every teacher could do to improve the quality of the learning of their students is to ask more questions that call for thinking. In one of our tests of creative thinking ability, we ask subjects to ask divergent questions, questions that are thought-provoking rather than questions that call only for facts. Most teachers find difficulty in doing this. Although they know that they are not supposed to ask factual questions, most of their questions still call only for reproduction of textbook facts. Analysis of questions asked in the classroom and on examinations indicate that about 90 percent of such questions deal only with the recognition or reproduction of textbook information.

Means and Standard Deviations of Pre- and Post-Test Scores on Fluency, Flexibility, Originality, and Elaboration on the Minnesota Tests of Creative Thinking (Non-Verbal Forms A and B) by Third Grade Pupils in Creative Movement Class

VARIABLE	PRE-TEST		POST-TEST		t RATIO
	MEAN	STAND. DEV.	MEAN	STAND. DEV.	
Fluency	15.57	4.79	21.55	5.64	8.318[a]
Flexibility	12.29	3.89	16.12	3.66	6.937[a]
Originality	13.81	5.19	27.19	8.94	10.750[a]
Elaboration	36.24	16.02	38.48	14.11	1.169

[a]Gain is significant at better than the .001 level.

6.   BUILD ONTO THE LEARNING SKILLS THAT YOUR PUPILS HAVE

There are many discontinuities in our educational system, but the most glaring and upsetting ones occur when the child enters school for the first time, between the third and fourth grades, and between the sixth and seventh grades. It shows up in many of our tests of creative thinking when we find drops rather than gains or even plateaus in the developmental curves. The most disturbing element in this problem is the apparent rise in personality disturbance behavior problems, and inability to learn and achieve in school.

Even when children first enter school, they have already developed a variety of skills for learning. They already know how to learn by experimenting, manipulating objects, rearranging them in different ways, singing, drawing, dancing, fantasy, storytelling, playmaking, and the like. It is quite likely that there would be fewer difficulties in learning and development if teachers made use of these learning skills and grafted education onto them, gradually building up the repertoire of learning skills rather than suddenly demanding that things be learned in ways strange to the child. This technique should be used all the way up the educational ladder.

7.   GIVE OPPORTUNITIES FOR LEARNING IN CREATIVE WAYS

Man seems to prefer to learn creatively, by exploring, questioning, experimenting, testing, and modifying ideas or solutions. Generally, however, the schools operate on the principle that it is cheaper to teach by authority. Our studies suggest, however, that many things now taught by authority can actually be learned more effectively and economically if they are learned creatively. Some individuals have strong preferences for learning in creative ways, learn a great deal if permitted to learn in these ways, and make little progress when we insist that they learn by authority. This means that we may be able to educate to a higher degree many people whom we have not been very successful in educating—our dropouts and school failures.

A variety of experiments show that as teachers vary the way in which children are encouraged to learn, different types of children in terms of mental abilities become the star learners or nonlearners. Traditional measures of mental age or intelligence correlate more highly with measures of achievement when knowledge is acquired by authority than when acquired creatively. Measures of originality and the like correlate more highly with measures of achievement when knowledge is acquired creatively than when acquired by authority.

REFERENCES

Jablonski, J. R. "Developing Creative Research Performance in Public School Children." In C. W. Taylor (ed.), *Widening Horizons in Creativity.* New York: John Wiley & Son, Inc., 1964.

Torrance, E. P. *Guiding Creative Talent.* Englewood Cliffs, N.J.: Prentice-Hall, Inc., 1962.

Torrance, E. P. *Education and the Creative Potential.* Minneapolis: University of Minnesota Press, 1963.

Torrance, E. P. *Rewarding Creative Behavior: Experiments in Classroom Creativity.* Englewood Cliffs, N.J.: Prentice-Hall, Inc., 1965.

The Movement Education Approach to Teaching in English Elementary Schools

SHIRLEY HOWARD

Movement education is a dynamic aspect of the total education program in England. Since its inception some twenty-five years ago, when movement education was first introduced to physical education in the elementary schools, the concept has developed in breadth and depth. The approach is now typical in elementary schools throughout the country. In secondary schools also, applications of the movement concepts have developed in both gymnastics and dance. Professional education programs in colleges are using movement education concepts in developing the personal skills of prospective teachers. The approach is widely advocated as a basis for instruction in physical education at both the elementary and secondary school levels.

The widespread adoption of the concepts of movement education by British educators is easy to understand when the approach is examined in terms of current educational philosophy. First, the individual development of each student is paramount. Every student has many opportunities to experience satisfaction from successful use of his body. Thus, success contributes to the improved self-confidence of the student, enhances his self-image, and provides the basis for his seeking more challenging tasks. The problem-solving type of approach popular today in curriculum planning for many teaching fields is the basic method used in the English approach to movement education. It requires total involvement of students in their own learning situation. In this approach students structure their own movements, within the restrictions of the problem, in ways which are meaningful to them, which enables each student to develop understanding and appreciation of movement as well as to improve his movement skills. Creativity is encouraged, because there is no single response to the problems.

The English movement education approach is centered around concepts in three areas: the use of the body (what moves), the use of space (where you move), and the quality of the movement (how you move). Themes to develop concepts of body awareness include transfer of weight, reception of weight, and shaping movements by such means as curling, stretching, and twisting. In addition to individual work, body use is developed through partner and group work in problems involving matching movements, contrasting movements, meeting and parting, and passing around, over, and under. Ability to use a variety of directions and levels serves as the core for spatial concepts. The quality of movement is described in terms of three factors: the "strength" of the movement as characterized by strong or light; the "time," characterized by quick, slow, acceleration or deceleration; and "flow," characterized by continuous, broken, successive, or simultaneous movement.

The teacher using the movement approach to physical education presents a problem emphasizing a single concept or, with older students, a combination of concepts. Each student then responds with movements that enable him to improve control of his body while also expanding his understanding of how this concept affects his ability to move. The problem-solving situation enables each student to gain satisfaction from moving within his own capacities.

In elementary schools, as well as in secondary schools and professional preparation programs at the college level, these movement experiences are further developed in relation to apparatus or what the British call modern educational gymnastics. Initially, students are given free choice of how they use the apparatus, both Olympic type and a variety of other interesting pieces. They are encouraged to move continuously, still with free choice of movement. Gradually the students are directed toward supporting and suspending their bodies on different parts of the apparatus and toward developing a variety of ways for mounting, dismounting, and moving on the apparatus. The teacher then further structures problems by specifying the path of the movement, the types of movement, or the quality of movement. This progression is designed to improve body management, confidence, and initiative in movement.

A feature of the excellent gymnastic programs in England is the abundance of apparatus available in even the smallest, most remote schools. In elementary schools apparatus is generally found both indoors and outdoors. Frequently it has been constructed so that it is portable and can easily be moved by small children. In harmony with the emphasis of the movement approach on student initiative and problem solving, British gymnasium equipment is highly flexible in arrangement. Students of all ages are able and encouraged to arrange and rearrange the equipment to suit their particular needs. Many pieces of apparatus are installed in the gymnasium on ceiling tracks; climbing ropes and vertical poles are quickly and efficiently moved into use. Other heavy pieces, such as horizontal beams and bar arrangements, are on a pivotal axis with anchor plates on the floor. Portable connecting bars and beams further extend the variety of possible arrangements.

Parallel to modern educational gymnastics, modern educational dance has developed from movement education in the elementary schools and in the girls program at the secondary and college levels. As in gymnastics, the emphasis is on freedom of movement as well as on creative and expressive movement response to dance stimuli. Dance themes are developed from music, rhythm instruments, and dramatic content. Variety in movement responses by children appears to be related to the variety of movement experiences which have preceded the introduction of dance. In the elementary schools, classroom activities of art, music, and creative writing are frequently integrated with the dance activities.

The applications of movement education to ball handling and game skills are not as widespread as are the applications to dance and gymnastics. In many elementary schools, educational gymnastics occupies the physical education session two of the five periods a week, while one period is devoted to games, including ball skills; one period is devoted to rhythms; and one is spent on athletics (track and field). Some of the teachers are able to apply the problem-solving approach to the entire curriculum; others use the movement education approach for educational gymnastics but return to traditional teaching methods for the other areas of the curriculum.

In general, the physical education program is enhanced by the large variety and quantity of equipment available for instructional use. Balls of varied size and type, paddles, jump ropes, bean bags, hoops, stilts, and wands provided each student maximal activity during each class period.

In the ball handling lessons observed, the children showed amazing ability both in dodging and in ball control. A representative lesson began with individual practice in tossing and catching, each child with his own ball. The children then threw to moving partners; children and balls were going in all directions, but the children seldom dropped the ball, touched one another, or hit anyone with a ball. The boys then demonstrated many football (soccer) skills which had been developed from such problem-solving tasks as stopping the ball with different parts of the body, putting the ball into the air from the floor without using the hands, passing the ball with the feet, and keeping the ball in the air with different parts of the body. Many of the boys could keep the ball in the air for a great length of time with their heads and showed amazing skill with their feet in all the techniques one would see in a professional game. The girls then demonstrated their skills with the ball. They first worked individually, keeping the ball in the air with their hands without catching and throwing, demonstrating beautiful over-head volleys with very little movement of the feet and excellent extension. They then worked in groups of three volleying the ball back and forth and while moving about the room.

The skill with which the boys and the girls handled the balls was an outgrowth of carefully structured problem-solving experiences and was accomplished without specific instruction as to how to do it. The skills gained are only later put to use in game situations.

Swimming skills are also developed from general movement experiences. Children learn to relax in the water and propel themselves through the water prior to any specific stroke analysis. Shallow, portable swimming pools are a recent addition to many elementary school facilities. Some times these pools are small enough to be placed in an empty classroom. In some cases, children change clothes in their classroom and go outdoors to a pool. A classroom teacher, who is interested and skilled in swimming, conducts the teaching for the school. Parent associations often raise the money for construction of the pools; the school systems support the maintenance of the facilities.

Another exciting application of the movement approach was observed in a film of a special school for severely physically handicapped children. The program utilized a positive approach, emphasizing the development of physical skills in spite of the varying restrictions of each student's physical capacities. A teen-age boy, with limited use of his legs, moved with ease when walking on his hands.

Generally, the students used apparatus and executed skills far beyond our expectations.

In considering the values of movement education in England, there was much agreement among the participants in the workshop. Generally, a high proficiency in body management skills was observed along with a freedom of movement. Students exhibited considerable interest and involvement in their movement experiences. Each student had many opportunities to experience success in movement because of the individualized nature of the instructional process. Physical fitness was highly developed and a natural outcome of the continuous movement and vigorous action inherent in this approach to teaching. The extent to which potential values were realized, of course, varied with individual teachers. Discipline problems were not seen; because children were so interested and so deeply involved and because they had opportunity to perform at their own level, there was no question of maintaining discipline.

The movement education approach in England is fully supported by the school systems through the provision of a daily instructional program and an abundance of apparatus and small equipment. Supervisory assistance is available on request, and in-service workshop opportunities are provided by the school systems.

Selected reactions of the participants summarize the observations made in England and reveal their stimulating effect on the American delegation.

"The student learns to respect his own abilities as well as the abilities of others."

"The movement approach seemed to draw out the shy, self-conscious child and lead him to other experiences."

"Children are not afraid to express their emotions."

"Continuous activity was emphasized throughout the lessons."

"All the children felt success in what they were doing."

"The major contribution to learning is that movement education tends to develop a positive self-concept."

"The sense of adventure, daring, creativity, and ability to handle themselves on large apparatus impressed me as I watched the five- to seven-year-olds."

The Cargo Net
John S. Hichwa

A cargo net is a new and creative piece of apparatus which excites and motivates primary and intermediate aged children to climb, balance, stretch, swing, and hang. It provides an opportunity to explore in a self-initiated and creative manner and gives each child a better idea of his own movement capabilities. There may be other cargo nets, but ours is unique in that it may be set up and used in a variety of ways.

Initially, the children should be allowed to explore and experiment on the net with as few limitations as possible. This self-initiated exploration satisfies the child's compelling desire to try something new and see what the cargo net is like.

Because the cargo net involves several children at the same time, and one child's movement will affect the movement of the others, the following suggestions could serve as guides in introducing the net to a physical education class:

1. Establish an atmosphere which will stimulate the children to meaningfully explore the many possibilities of the net.
2. Limit the height the children may climb during their first experience on the net.
3. Provide adequate matting under the cargo net.

These safety precautions are important; however, most children will only experiment at that level of skill in which they feel safe and secure.

Once the students have had this initial experience of exploration, the teacher may make suggestions so as to stimulate the children to try new skills. For example, he may say:

"In how many different directions can you move?"

"Let's see who can stretch and cover up as much space as possible."

"How many different shapes can you find formed by the ropes of the net? Can you crawl through any one of them? Can you crawl through one of the spaces and climb on the outside of the net?"

"Who can move so that you will go over or under someone?"

"How high can you climb? How low?"

"See if you can move, keeping as much distance as possible from one another."

"See how close you can get to one another without touching each other."

"Find a spot on the net. Who can move to a spot furthest from you?"

"How fast can you move on the net? How slow?"

"How can you swing on the net or be swung?"

"Can you climb the net using only your hands?"

"Can you climb horizontally across the net using only your hands?"

"With the net in a basket shape, find a stable position in the center of the basket. Can children standing on the floor shake you out?"

"Can you find a place on the cargo net and lay down as if you were in a hammock?"

"How many different ways can you find to get on or off the cargo net?"

"Can you do a hip circle mount or dismount on the net?"

The cargo net is both physically and emotionally challenging. It provides a stimulus for instant action.

In the self-initiated and guided phases of introducing the cargo net, it is important that the teacher and student communicate as much as possible. Let the children explain what they are doing and encourage a constant verbal and visual exchange of ideas.

Once the children become fully accustomed to the net, more specific activities may be initiated. For example you may want to have a round tug-o-war, have one group of children swing another, use the net in an obstacle course, or play "space tag" on the net.

Specific activities are fun, but children learn a great deal and enjoy self-initiated exploration. It is important that you revert back to this phase of teaching frequently, particularly with younger children.

The cargo net provides the children with the opportunity to explore on a three dimensional piece of equipment which moves as they move. The students discover depth and direction as well as develop basic spacial skills and strength. It allows them to create and discover basic movements at their own rate. Their courage and self-confidence is challenged. Their imagination is stimulated. Their natural interests and instincts are aroused.

Children need to discuss, to explore, to experiment, and to understand the basic elements of movement. The cargo net can aid each child to recognize and develop a kinesthetic awareness of these elements which include:

1. *Space*—discovering its various dimensions
   up-down
   forward-backward
   twisted-straight
   flexible-curved
   direct path-indirect path
   big-small
2. *Time*—learning how it affects movement
   fast-slow and all speeds in between

3. *Force*—experimenting with it and its effects
    strong-weak
    push-pull
    tense-relaxed
4. *Flow*—feeling the pleasures of moving from one skill to
    another with ease and fluency.

Cargo Net
Capers
John Kautz

A cargo net is used to load a variety of freight aboard a ship. In school it can become a new and useful piece of equipment that serves as a fertile medium for exposing students to movement exploration in physical education.

When you first see children climbing a cargo net, it may remind you of spiders climbing across their gossamer webs. As the children reach with hands and feet for rungs which suddenly no longer maintain their original position, this activity provides them with an experience in space relations. Motivation to succeed increases when several youngsters are climbing at once.

In addition to learning to cope with this self-generated movement of the net, the children have a chance to explore, create, and discover basic body movements. Further, each child's strength, balance, agility, coordination, and climbing abilities are developed.

Initial Approach

While children are first trying out the net, put minimum restrictions on their enthusiasm. Let them decide what height they wish to achieve in their first undertaking. Originality and eagerness to discuss their climbing ideas with each other will become apparent, as they gain confidence.

You can further promote such discussion by suggesting other means of exploration, such as: Show me the different directions in which you might travel. How long can you make yourself? (Most pupils react by hanging by their hands or attempting to stretch out horizontally.) How small can you make yourself on the net? (Curling up will be demonstrated.) Can Ruth and Debbie change places without touching? Can anyone move so that he will go over or under somebody else? Is it possible to climb up one side of the net and come down on the other side?

To develop other movements, arrange the net in a basket shape. Then cue the children with: What different ways are there to get on or off the net? How close can you get to the floor without touching it? Can you have two parts of your body on one side of the net and the remainder on the other side?

Specific Activities

Recognition—A challenge for second-grade pupils. In this game, teams form capital letters using trunks, arms, and legs. Divide the class into three or four teams. Each team is privately given a letter to form. They have one minute to discuss who will take what position in the formation. The remaining teams then vie to see which can guess the figure first. A right guess, one point. A wrong guess, subtract a point. Over a specified period of time each team forms an equal number of letters. Team with the most points at the end wins.

Grasshopper Rotation—The first pupil takes a position on the net near the bottom. Second pupil climbs over the first and assumes a position just above him. A third pupil advances over first and second players and becomes the top man. First player then advances over second and third players. This rotation continues with the lowest man always advancing to the top. When descending on either the original or opposite side of the net, the top man always climbs down over the other two and becomes bottom man.

Wiggleworm—With three or four children climbing simultaneously, each tries to weave in and out of the rungs as they ascend vertically.

Head Tag—With a large number of students on the net, one person is designated as "it." "It" attempts to touch another player on the head and when a player is touched, he becomes "it." In the meantime, all other players are scurrying about the net to avoid being in the area occupied by "it."

In all instances, take safety precautions. Place an ample supply of mats under the net. Ask no one to exceed his or her own personal limitations.

Installation of a cargo net can be done in any open area that has exposed beams or adequate overhead projections, for anchoring the net.

Hemp cargo nets of various sizes can be purchased from surplus stores or supply centers. The more pliable nylon nets can be ordered from the Sterling Net and Twine Company, 7 Oak Place, Montclair, New Jersey 07042, which sells nets by the square foot and will fill orders for specific sized nets. All that you need do is send in a diagram denoting the width and length you want. Your net will be made accordingly.

Physical Education in the Nursery School Program

BERNARD WOLF

The objectives of our nursery school physical education program are to offer the children an opportunity to develop a good attitude toward physical fitness, to exercise the large muscle areas of the body, and to gain poise, courage, and body control through enjoyable activities. The nursery school child needs to develop strength, endurance, speed, and agility through activities geared specifically to his level of development. Such activities as running and chasing, climbing, jumping, suspension, kicking, throwing, batting, and the many responses to rhythms are used in our program to help the child develop a well-coordinated flexible body.

The learning of motor skills will play an increasingly important part in the social life of children. We see in later grades that those with good motor skills are chosen first and those with poor skills chosen last, or not at all, with damaging social consequences. Our physical education program includes: games of low organization, free ball activity, marching, rhythmic activities of simple design, tumbling activities, physical fitness exercises, obstacle course, balance and coordination teaching activities, stunts—relays, "make believe" games or mimetics, and use of gym apparatus (flying rings, trapeze, chinning bar, and climbing rope).

A characteristic of this age group is that the child is farsighted and cannot focus quickly or accurately. To try to pitch a baseball and have him hit it would not be a good activity since he probably wouldn't see the ball until it had passed him. Instead, we play "baseball" by using a special batting "T". A six-inch or eight-inch rubber ball is placed on the "T" and hit with a light plastic bat.

A child's love of rhythm and desire to imitate may be utilized to provide valuable creative experiences for him. With a piano player your program can be more flexible and imaginative. If you must use records, plan in advance to avoid repetition; if the children learn the rhythmic response by rote, it is no longer a creative response.

Within the past two years a program of physical fitness has been initiated at the Community Center. The children learn to do various exercises including sit-ups, push-ups, leg raises, stretches, bend, squats, and an assortment of floor movements. Perfection in performance was not the aim since coordinations are developing slowly. The children especially enjoyed repeating, as loud as they wished, all the commands issued by the leader. One-syllable commands were issued, such as—up—down—front—back—to make them easy to repeat.

Since a child's heart and lungs are small in proportion to his height and weight, it is important to plan for rest after a vigorous activity. During this time a quiet circle game can be played.

Although the attention span of young children is short, love of repetition prolongs interest. In a game like "Cat & Mouse" it is not uncommon that interest will last for ten minutes. Each class should be broken into small groups so that each child can be a participant as well as an active spectator. Imitating animals, western heroes, and make-believe characters can exercise the large muscles as well as the creative imagination. Large muscle activity can be repeated through stunts such as the wheelbarrow, the monkey walk, and the frog jump.

Special Equipment and Apparatus

Apparatus designed especially for the nursery school age can be purchased or constructed. It must be both strong and durable and meet all safety specifications. Wooden articles should be sanded smooth and brightly colored. Metal apparatus should be free from sharp edges, built so as not to shift or slide while in use. Almost any piece of apparatus can be constructed at a fraction of the price of a purchased piece of equipment. A set of balance blocks and boards, used in developing coordination, sells for sixteen dollars. The same equipment can be constructed by the building supervisor or maintenance staff for $1.50 to $2.00 including paint and one hour of labor. A piano is a useful item for use in the rhythmic program, but if one is not available, a record player can be used. A portable record player will not have the volume to carry the sound in a large room or gym. A portable public address system with a record player attachment is needed.

Suggestions for Starting a Program

Listed below are suggestions for conducting a physical education program for nursery school children.

1. Know the game, story, or rhythm before attempting to teach it.

2. Correlate activities with classroom interests wherever possible.

3. Remember that children want action; don't stall.

4. Consider the physiological condition of the participants. Alternate strenuous games with semi-active and quiet games. The game program should not be an endurance contest.

5. Do not limit your choice of games to those using balls and other equipment.

6. Feature some games without equipment so that the participants will be able to play them when no equipment is available.
7. Use as little time as possible when getting ready for a game.
8. Have all children participate.
9. Make explanations quick and concise.
10. Participate in games with the children at every opportunity.
11. Expect and demand attention.
12. Know what you're going to do and how you're going to do it. Preparation for the game period requires as much thought and planning as planning for a regular nursery school classroom session.
13. Be sure you have all your game equipment ready beforehand so that you can move smoothly and swiftly from one game to the next.

Conducting the Game

It may be necessary and desirable for the game leader to take part in the game at the outset in order to get the ball rolling. If so, he should play a minor and inconspicuous role so that he may be able to eliminate himself and work with another group if necessary. Terminate the game while the interest is high. Do not overplay the game until interest lags. Have another equally good game on hand. If participants like the game, they will come back to it in the future.

Safety Factors to Consider

Gym shoes or sneakers must be worn in the gymnasium. This prevents slipping and sliding and can prevent serious accidents in the program. The parents are told, during the registration period, that each child must have a pair of gym shoes on hand at the Center. When gym time comes, the children all go to their special cabinet and take their sneakers out in preparation for the program.

Be sure that the gym floor is swept clean and is in a smooth condition before the children arrive. Many of the activities include crawling, sliding, and mass floor activities.

In activities with special apparatus, such as the trapeze or flying rings, it is important that the teachers assisting in the program are made aware of the safety factors involved. Teachers should be used as spotters in tumbling and in the use of special apparatus where needed. In working with the trapeze or flying rings, the teacher's hand should be placed under the child's body, so as to break his fall if he lets go of the apparatus. A large mat should also be placed under the apparatus.

We feel that by helping children to grow in coordination and agility, to master movements and skills, to handle play equipment, to perform athletic feats, and to develop social qualities such as teamwork, sharing, playing fair, learning to lead and to follow, our nursery school program prepares them for a happy and active childhood.

These Are Your Children
GLADYS GARDNER JENKINS

You who have specialized in physical education understand the physical development of children and the desirable ways of helping them to achieve physical fitness. You are aware of the values of a physically active life. You recognize that continued exercise and use of the body is essential for physical health and that recreation is essential for a balanced life.

Yet, in your field as well as mine, we are seeking for the reasons why the eager, active participation of the primary school child too frequently turns into apathy toward physical activity and participation in sports and games. By the time they enter high school many once eager youngsters have become spectators. They cheer lustily, criticize the umpire, shout their disapproval, but no longer have an interest in active sports. Even the bicycle has been put away, the car is in vogue, and one never walks if one can ride.

I cannot present an authoritative solution to this problem, but I want to share with you some pertinent insights from the field of child development.

As teachers and recreation leaders we strive to teach children the things we feel are important, but we realize that we cannot *make* a child learn. He has to want to learn what we want to teach, for only in this way can he make the knowledge offered a part of himself.

Dorothy Gardner, in the fine book *Feelings and Learning,* says that "the basis of learning is emotion ... there is no intellectual interest which does not spring from the need to satisfy feelings."[1] Any education must always take into account the emotions. We as teachers have observed "how often a distressed or irritable child passes into a mood of calm cheerfulness when he finds an outlet for his feelings in the joy of discovery and mastery."[2] In reverse, we have observed how an overanxious, discouraged, or tense child is blocked in his ability to learn, whether it be throwing a ball or reading. To make a child want to learn, three questions must be considered.

---

[1]Dorothy E. M. Gardner, "Emotions, A Basis for Learning," *Feelings and Learning,* Association for Childhood Education International (Washington, D.C.: The Association, 1965), 34.
[2]*Ibid.*

What Kind of a Child Is He?

We are all aware of the many differences among children. A longitudinal study of 231 children whose psychological development has been followed since their birth[3] reveals that certain characteristics shown by babies in relating to their environment tend to persist in later childhood, thus giving an indication of the individual's temperament. Temperament is defined as the basic style which characterizes a person's behavior. The following differences in behavior are of significance:

Activity level. Some babies from early infancy were much more active than others. Even when they slept they moved more than other infants.

Regularity of biological functions. Feeding, bowel movements, sleep followed rhythmic patterns. Mothers could plan the day's activities around the regularity of some babies. Others were irregular and unpredictable.

Approach or withdrawal as a characteristic response to a new situation. Some babies had no trouble with new experiences such as the first bath, new food, new places. Others screamed or reacted negatively.

Adaptability to change in routine. Some babies shifted easily and quickly to a changing schedule. They could alter their behavior to fit the mother's pattern. With others a change of routine consistently brought about fussing or crying; only with difficulty and much repetition were mothers successful in introducing a new pattern. Some babies did not adapt at all, and the mother had to adjust to the child's pattern rather than continue an unsuccessful and upsetting struggle.

Level of sensory threshold. Some babies were more disturbed by light, noises, being touched, being wet or dry. The response to pain varied markedly.

Positive or negative mood. Some babies characteristically gurgled and smiled frequently; others tended to whimper and fuss. Some were passive and neutral, not reacting to what was happening.

Intensity of response. Some children expressed much more energy than others in their behavior. One cried lustily when he was hungry, another softly. The child of low intensity smiled gently when pleased; the more vigorous one chortled, gurgled, and kicked when happy.

Distractibility. Some babies seemed able to concentrate better than others—no amount of diversion easily altered their

[3]Alexander Thomas and Others, *Behavioral Individuality in Early Childhood,* New York: New York University Press, 1963; Stella Chess and Others, *Your Child Is a Person,* New York: Viking Press, 1965.

behavior. The distractible child, however, could be diverted by a toy or by being picked up or talked to.

Persistence and attention span. Some infants were able to pursue an activity in the face of difficulties or to resume it after an interruption, such as sucking persistently at a nipple with small holes, though little milk was coming through. Others gave up quickly. A year later the same babies stuck to one toy for a long period, while the less persistent changed toys frequently.

How do these findings relate to the response of the children we teach? It may be much more difficult for one child to sit still or conform to the demands of the schoolroom than another. It would make a difference on the playground or in the gymnasium in terms of the enthusiasm with which a child takes part. The *slow warmer-upper* could be frightened away from willing, active participation if he were pushed into a new activity or group before he felt able to take the step. He may have to watch for awhile. The *highly active* child may be eager but not able to settle down enough to listen to directions. The *persistent, nondistractible* youngster may plug away and not want to move into another activity. He may find it hard to stop, hard to let go. The child with an *intense response* may be more vulnerable in situations involving competition. He may be more hurt by teasing and taunts. He may hit out at another child when he is upset or angry. The child whose *sensory level is low* may be disturbed by noise and contact sports or by being shoved around. Little physical hurts may seem bigger and produce genuine pain.

An undesirable cycle of interaction may arise between child and teacher if their temperaments differ greatly. A teacher may be drawn more toward one child than another, showing this in her behavior as she speaks or works with different children. It is easy to be pleasant and encouraging with the child whose temperament clicks with ours, and irritable or impatient with the one whose behavior bothers or annoys.

To motivate children to learn we must accept the fact of basic temperamental differences, sometimes modifying our approach for the children not readily adaptable to our program. Without sufficient flexibility, we will make these youngsters lose interest in the physical activity which many of them so sorely need.

Even though we can intellectually accept the theory of individual differences, we need to go one step further into the realm of values and ask ourselves, *Whom do I value? Whom do I feel it is worthwhile to teach?*

A recent study by Dr. Bondel of the Bureau of Child Guidance in New York City showed that teachers rewarded the conforming child rather than met the needs of the intellectually demanding child and that they often underestimated the more inhibited child, the "quiet one." I wonder whether in the gymnasium or on the playground it is not the physically competent child who is favored, approved, and rewarded, rather than those who perhaps are equally eager but less competent. Maybe these less physically skillful youngsters need encouragement most, yet are too often overlooked in a large, active class.

We need to examine our feelings about the children we teach. Do we genuinely value every child, whatever his ability or temperament? Do we really care and want to motivate each child to do his best?

What Can He Achieve?

Today emphasis is shifting from *competitive* achievement toward *self-achievement*—evident even at the university level. Much uneasiness prevails over the intense competition for grades, which seems to result in a loss of desire to learn for the sake of knowledge.

For many years we have been burdened with the cliche that we live in a competitive world and our children must, at any cost to themselves, get used to competition. In part, this is certainly true, but the statement does not take into account two very important considerations. It is only in childhood, particularly during school days, that children are expected to compete with no chance of ever winning. *Yet the essence and challenge of competition is that you may have a chance to win.* Even in a golf tournament handicaps are given to try to meet inequities in experience and skill. On the other hand, in the classroom and on the playground the skillful are too often pitted against those of less physical or mental ability or opportunity.

Secondly, a child must experience a degree of success before he can take competition in stride. *He must have some self-confidence.* Competition in which the child consistently loses is poor preparation for life in a competitive world. The ability to take real competition comes slowly. It is built upon self-respect and self-confidence in some area.

Six- and seven-year-olds, and even some eights, are so engrossed in trying to find themselves in the world of school that they have little emotional leeway for competition or criticism. They all want to be first. This drive is intense. It is such an integral part of themselves that primary grade children are easily pushed into cheating, using alibis, failing to observe the rules of the game—if this is the only way they can win. A young child will often burst into tears if competition is made too important a part of the game.

By the time a youngster is nine or ten he is ready to enter into competitive situations with more zest, providing the competition is among near enough equals so that he has a chance of being a winner or being on the winning side. If competition becomes more important than playing the game, as it sometimes does in Little League, a child of this age does not yet have enough emotional reserve to handle the tension. He may go to pieces under a strain which is too much too soon. *He is not a poor loser but an overtaxed child.*

The child who always loses in competition, or is not good enough to be on a team, will have little motive to go on playing the game. Could this be one reason why so many of our boys and girls gradually lose interest in sports as they reach an age when team play and winning become increasingly stressed? Do we also tend to leave the brunt of bearing the disappointment of physical inadequacy upon the shoulders of the less competent child by saying, "He must find his level or place"?

As teachers we must help a child understand his strengths and limitations in a realistic fashion so that his self-respect remains intact and his strengths are discovered. Also, a child should not be exposed to a barrage of unfavorable comments or rejection from other boys and girls. Children in the excitement of wanting to win can be cruel, and many children are badly hurt and permanently damaged by the taunts of others. We must teach children the meaning of individual differences and to help them accept those of less ability.

A physical education program fails in its purpose if, in an overemphasis upon winning, it widens the rift between the child who is physically skillful and the one who is less apt. In the elementary school above all, it is the task of the physical education teacher or recreation director to help children develop sportsmanship, playing for the sake of the game, never calling the loser names or making a child the scapegoat if his team loses.

Once we understand how a child feels when he is constantly not quite good enough, we will pay more attention to *self-achievement.* It is doing one's best which should win approval.

Developing leadership is another important part of *self-achievement.* The competent child needs personal self-achievement. The competent child needs personal recognition as well to foster his growth. But sometimes we forget that it takes time to develop potential leadership. Even though the children may have chosen their own leader, it is rarely wise to leave an elementary school child in charge of a group for long. Even a popular child with leadership ability is not yet mature enough to handle all the situations which arise among youngsters, or to be sufficiently aware of the needs and feelings of the more vulnerable children. They are still learners in the art of leadership. Without wise guidance a youngster may use his role as "boss" to dominate the others—which can destroy the value of the leadership experience. It is as important to help the leader to lead as to help the less skillful child become part of the group.

How Does a Child Feel About Himself?

The more we learn about children through research and clinical studies, the more we realize the importance of the picture a child develops of himself. A child gains his self-image from those around him. If he finds himself liked—if parents, teachers and other boys and girls respond to him positively—he can be free of anxiety about himself, free to learn within the framework of his abilities. But when a child has experienced too much failure and discouragement, when the expectations of what he must do have exceeded his capacities, background, or experience, he begins to doubt his personal worth. When this happens, anxiety crowds out the positive feelings and he may hit out against a world which is depriving him of confidence. Such a child may call attention to himself and to his need in undesirable ways—fighting, bullying, taunting—or he may withdraw into himself and cease trying.

Sometimes we are so concerned about following our lesson plan for the day that we do not see the situations causing children to develop a poor self-image. What does it mean to a child to hear someone say: "Who will take Jimmy—we don't want him!"

or to hear the whispered comment: "We don't want her on our side!"

or to stand embarrassed and dispirited because time after time he is the last one chosen.

or to be taunted for losing the race or hitting out because he was not as skillful as the others and winning had become too important?

It is tough to be left standing while everyone else is chosen. This child may be the very one most in need of team sports and fun in games with others. It may be the obese child who should be helped to learn how to use his body. It might be the timid child who needs assistance in becoming less fearful of physical activity. And don't forget the slow warmer-upper who finds it hard to learn the new game or move into a new activity situation. It is such children who are likely to turn to more solitary, less active pursuits rather than be humiliated again and again. The picture of oneself can bear only so much defeat.

But it is not always the less skillful child who suffers too much anxiety or develops a false picture of himself. Dr. Sarason in *Anxiety in Elementary School Children* reports that many teachers in his study did not recognize anxiety when it occurred in the bright and alert student. He found that children who were doing well often thought of themselves as failures. The child whom everyone expects to win the race or make the home run sometimes suffers under excessive strain. He, too, may become overanxious.

This does not mean that we should always make things easy but, rather, that we set goals permitting each child to experience some measure of success. Children of all levels of ability need to learn how to work hard, play hard, put out effort, and use their inner tensions to press toward accomplishing something.

Children like to be challenged—but the challenge must be reasonable for the child. If we watch a child learning to throw a ball or use a bat we see effort going into his first attempts. He may screw up his face as he uses his whole body to throw, or overtense his muscles, or stand rigidly as he first tries to bat. He is anxious. But this is his effort. A bit of anxiety directed outward toward the accomplishment of a task he feels ready to tackle will not hurt him. He is eager to learn. He is trying hard. On the other hand, if he fails and tries too hard too many times because he is not yet ready for this experience, then he may come to feel that he is no good. If this happens, the anxiety which was wholesome when it was siphoned off into successful activity becomes unwholesome. The anxiety of constant failure may pervade a child's feelings and instead of leading toward action it may block his desire to try again and indeed block his later ability to master the skill. It is the second kind of anxiety which we need to check as children are being taught the skills and games of the physical education program. We must be aware of the child's readiness to be able to master with some success the skill we are trying to teach. Occasional failure balanced by success is not harmful but to be expected; continuous failure can destroy a child's picture of himself as an acceptable person.

One cannot separate the child's self-image from his sense of self-achievement. A child with limited capacity can still be helped to succeed sufficiently within his own abilities. Even though knowing that he cannot achieve in every area or as well as others, he will then not be overly discouraged.

Feelings affect motivation and learning, and you and I must take them into account. The difference between the person who instructs and the person who is a real teacher lies in the ability to recognize the importance of a child's feelings about himself. We are really teaching if each child can leave our group holding his head high with self-respect and feeling that he is a person of worth.

BIBLIOGRAPHY

Association for Childhood Education International. *Feelings and Learning.* Washington, D.C.: The Association, 1965.

Chess, Stella. *Your Child Is a Person.* New York: Viking Press, 1965.

Erikson, Erik H. *Childhood and Society.* Rev. ed. New York: W. W. Norton & Co., Inc., 1964.

Jenkins, Gladys Gardner. *Helping Children Reach Their Potential.* Chicago: Scott, Foresman & Company, 1961.

————, and others. *These Are Your Children.* Chicago: Scott, Foresman & Company, 1953.

Sarason, Seymor B. *Anxiety in Elementary School Children.* New York: John Wiley & Sons, Inc., 1960.

Thomas, Alexander, and Others. *Behavioral Individuality in Early Childhood.* New York: New York University Press, 1963.

Helping Youngsters Read Through Physical Education Experiences

ANTHONY F. PEGNIA

It is the general belief that elementary school children love physical activity. They enjoy rhythmic skills, games of low organization and imitating both people and animals. It is also an accepted fact that reading and its related skills are usually taught in the first grade. The basic skill of vocabulary development through the recognition of sight words; and the various comprehension skills are usually the major teaching objectives of grades one and two. Various sub-skills must also be in evidence before a child can meet with success in his initial reading experience.

Many problems arise in this beginning stage of learning to read. Motivating the child and keeping his interest sustained so he becomes actively involved in the learning process are two major problems the classroom teacher faces. This personal involvement must be present so that the necessary skills can be accepted and assimilated by the child in a positive manner.

Because experiences in physical education possesses by their very nature an intrinsic motivational factor, children are excited, interested and are willing to participate. If this assumption is considered to be true, then the expert in physical education can and should motivate children to enjoy reading. This can be done by the physical educator using a few simple techniques. The experiences he provides can be used to develop an interest and pleasure in reading.

One technique the physical educator can use is the experience chart. The experience chart and its important use to the student, the classroom teacher and the physical educator can be explained by citing two very common teaching situations.

The game Freeze and the experience chart which followed the actual playing of the game were taught to a first grade class.

The rules of the game are:

1. On the signal "Go" from the instructor, children run to the right around the circle.
2. The children may pass another child, but they may not reverse their direction of running.
3. When the instructor blows the whistle, all children must come to a full-stop, stop any noise, and look at the instructor.
4. Those failing to do so, or those who bump into another child when stopping, are out of the game for one turn.

After the youngsters had learned and played the game they were asked the following questions:

1. What did we do today?
2. What was the new game called?
3. How do we play Freeze?
4. Did we like this game?
5. Shall we play Freeze again?

The recorded responses were:

1. We played a new game today.
2. The game is called Freeze.
3. We run and stop.
4. We like to play Freeze.
5. We want to play Freeze again.

As each question was asked and the corresponding response given the sentence was written on the board then read first by an individual, next by the entire group. When the story was completed it was reread by the group. A title was then chosen for the story.

The second example relates to that part of physical education called movement exploration. The children were asked to name and demonstrate the different ways we could possibly jump. At the completion of the lesson the children were asked to cite the various ways we jumped.

The responses were recorded on the chalkboard and then later transferred to a chart. The responses again were read first by an individual and then by the entire class.

The responses given were:

1. one foot
2. two feet
3. forward
4. backward

5. sidewards
6. jump and stoop
7. jump and turn
  Animals Jump
1. dogs
2. cats
3. frogs
4. kangaroos

By providing the children with a pleasurable experience and following up the activity with a discussion of what had taken place, the children were able to see their thoughts and feelings take shape in the form of words and a story that could be retold and "read" often.

Through the use of the experience chart the special subject teacher is able to help children put into spoken and written words an experience unique to his particular field. The art and music teacher as well as the physical education instructor should recognize his ability to contribute to the development of and an interest in reading by the child. Each provides a highly diversified activity for the child with its own skills and vocabulary.

Track Endurance Training for Elementary School Children?

R. L. WICKSTROM

Running is a fundamental movement for children which is basically interesting and fun to do. Children run spontaneously and joyously until they become tired and then stop and rest. One could hardly argue with that kind of logic unless, of course, he were interested in other beneficial aspects of running. Running is one of the simplest and most effective ways of developing an important aspect of organic vigor; i.e., circulorespiratory endurance. If the child stops running when he tires, he will not get the stimulus necessary for the development of endurance. Hence, a dilemma. The problem would seem to be that of preserving the natural, enjoyable aspects of running and at the same time of providing enough stress to promote circulorespiratory endurance.

Proper Amount of Stress or Overload

Studies in child development show quite clearly the difficulty in determining the optimal amount of stress for the development of endurance in the elementary school child. Because of the great concern for the welfare of the child the tendency in the schools has been to underwork rather than to overstimulate the child in the area of endurance training. Cureton's work with boys has provided abundant evidence regarding the promotion of endurance in preadolescent and in adolescent boys. His findings suggest that the traditional elementary school physical education program is deficient by a large measure in providing endurance promoting activities. Rarely is the child worked too hard; more often he is not worked hard enough.

If track endurance training is to be used at the elementary school level it must be individualized far more than most activities are at this level. The tasks must be set in such a way that they create a challenge to each child without asking him to exceed his limits. It is possible to do this within the structure and organization of a typical class.

The Concept of Pace

When children run it is apparent most of them know only one pace, fast. Practically all of the games they play involve running at full speed so it is not too difficult to understand why children are strangers to the concept of variable pace. Since endurance work involves being able to continue running, the idea of running at slow speeds must be introduced and stressed. Those who have attempted to teach the concept of pace are familiar with the difficulty children have in grasping the idea and in controlling their automatic accelerators when working on running pace.

A useful first step in teaching the concept of pace is to explain and illustrate the differences between walking, jogging and running (possibly also sprinting). Then the instructor can concentrate on jogging or slow running and search for ways to implement this particular aspect of pace.

Essentially, jogging involves *short steps,* slow tempo, and minor movement of the arms and legs. It is easy and relaxing. Jogging in place can emphasize these points and set the children for a more advanced phase of pace training. Then the children can all get in a small circle facing the same direction and jog forward using the same basic form as jogging in place, except that *short steps* forward are taken. At this point, if the teacher could lead the children there would be assurance of a slow pace. Later the children would have to be given the opportunity to test their own sense of pace because, finally, it is an individual matter. Gradually the distance has to be increased but not the tempo. In this way pace can be taught without the significant involvement of the overload principle which is essential to the development of endurance in track. At this point it is *first things first,* and the problem of pace definitely is first.

The Concept of Overload

Children respond with more enthusiasm in a situation where they know what is happening to them and why they are doing a particular thing. This is especially true when the procedure is new and potentially stressful to the child. By its definition overload involves stress and needs to be explained. Included in the explanation might be something concerning the nature of endurance, how it develops over a period of time, why hard work is necessary when overload is used, how rest can be of value in endurance training, and how to recognize improvement. All of these points should not be discussed at the same time but rather as the situation requires further information. A course in exercise physiology is not required nor is the use of highly technical terms. The form of the explanation might be to relate the actual tasks or activity procedures to the expected improvement in performance. An instructor can show the concept of overload training by helping the children understand why they run one lap around the gym floor, walk one lap and then repeat four times. After several days of this when the number of repetitions is increased from four to five an actual implementation of the concept has been made. And the individual nature of overload is stressed by permitting each child to use his own pace.

The Setting of Goals

Children enjoy the challenge of a reasonable goal. If the teacher were to announce that the class would start practicing running and would increase the distance run each day until everyone in the class could run at least one-fourth of a mile without stopping, the challenge would be extended. In addition the procedure for meeting the challenge would be suggested and the procedure could be amplified as the training proceeded. The suggestion of one-fourth mile was for the purpose of illustration only. Every elementary school child probably could run that distance *without special practice* if the pace were sufficiently slow.

Goals can be arranged in such a way that they can be individualized and at the same time interject a satisfactory overload for the development of endurance. Each child should be concerned with his own performance and his previous efforts as well as the goal of the class. If there is an extreme range of development within the group, secondary goals or challenges can be employed.

A variation of goal setting as explained above is the task setting procedure used in movement exploration. It provides for individual response and at the same time has the entire class active doing the same sort of activity. The basic difference is seen in the pace being used by different children in the class. Some examples of kinds of tasks are included in the following:

1. Can you jog without stopping for 15 seconds?
2. Can you jog without stopping for 30 seconds?
3. Can you jog without stopping for 15 seconds and then do it again after a short rest?
4. Can you jog without stopping for 60 seconds?
5. Can you jog without stopping for one minute but at a faster pace than before?
6. Can you run fast for 10 seconds and then jog for one minute without stopping?

Etc. Etc. Etc.

Tasks can be arranged in series to be used on the same day or on consecutive days with the total amount of work plus the intensity of the work being progressively increased.

Other Track Training for Running Endurance

Running in place. When the space is restricted or the weather inclement, endurance training in track can continue. Running in place is basically not very interesting to children but with careful treatment of the situation it can become acceptable and effective.

1. Jog in place for a predetermined period of time. Increase the amount of time at regular intervals and encourage a faster pace by those who feel they can do it.

2. Jog in place for a set period of time, rest, then jog again and continue for a controlled number of repetitions.

3. Run in place for a predetermined number of steps and let each child keep track of the number of steps taken by one foot. He should try to decrease the amount of time required to do the set number of steps. Later the number of steps must be increased in accordance with the overload principle.

4. Run in place trying to increase the number of steps in a set period of time. Later the set period of time must be increased.

5. Run in place as fast as possible for a short period of time, rest, and repeat. The number of repetitions may be increased, the length of time the child is asked to run may be increased, or the amount of time devoted to rest may be decreased to provide an overload.

6. Run in place as fast as possible for a short period of time, jog for a rest variation and repeat the combination several times.

These can be quite difficult for elementary school children and must be used with considerable thought to the particular situation. Overwork at an early time is not only indefensible but is disastrous in terms of the response of the children to endurance training in track.

Running of Relays

The running of relays may be considered part of the regular track endurance training or may be used to inject a brief spirit of competition into the training. But in either case more than one brief spurt of maximum speed running must be required of each participant.

1. A continuous relay around a set course with no predetermined end. The number of team members would be determined by the distance, the speed of running and the amount of rest needed.
2. A shuttle relay with 4-10 legs run by each member of a group or team.
3. A shuttle relay in groups of three for a distance of 25 to 50 yards. Groups can be formed according to the speed and endurance of the individuals in the class. The speed can be less than full speed and at the same time be very useful in promoting endurance.

Milethon and Variations

This is an advanced type of training in which significant time or distance demands are made on the children. Cureton used this with glowing success in the many years the fitness program for children has operated at the University of Illinois.

1. Increase the distance run in a set period of time. For individualizing this type of training the children may run or walk but the total distance covered in a set period of time by each is recorded. The set period of time is increased over the period of training.
2. Increase the distance run in a set period of time with only the distance covered while running being counted in the child's record.

Summary

Elementary school children can become involved in endurance training in connection with track activities if the procedure is carefully controlled. It requires a change from speed running with frequent rests when tired, which is quite natural for the child, to a slower pace continued over a protracted period of time even when tired. Children are not adults and must not be trained as though they were. By appealing to the interests and needs of the child, the instructor can challenge him to improve his endurance significantly and have fun at the same time. With a little encouragement elementary school children will develop the ability to jog at least a half mile and most will be able to do one to several miles.

Jumping Builds Coordination
Doyice J. Cotton
Jumping rope is an old playground standby. It can be fun for the students and easier for the teacher to supervise if a little extra time is spent in learning the skills involved in turning and jumping the rope.

Teaching Tips
1. Keep the jumping lines short by using several ropes.
2. Don't allow one player to jump for a long time while others stand and watch.
3. Change turners frequently so they get jumping activity and others get turning practice.
4. No "hot" jumping until children are sufficiently skilled.
5. Take time to teach students how to turn a long rope effectively. This will give you freedom to help less skilled jumpers.

Equipment
For a class of 30, you need four 10- to 12-foot jump ropes and at least fifteen 5- to 6-foot jump ropes. Use sash rope of 1/2- or 5/8-inch diameter and tie a knot at each end of the rope to prevent raveling.

Group Jump Rope
Use a long rope, rolling up the excess and holding it in turning hand or free hand so the rope is 8 to 10 feet long. The turners should not be further apart than necessary. The rope will turn smoothly if the turners work in rhythm. Counting or chanting "up, up, up ... " will be helpful in establishing and maintaining this rhythm. Young students will probably find it easier to turn with a whole-arm motion. Older ones may prefer to turn with a wrist motion. To keep the rope from getting too high, the turners should be sure it hits the ground on each swing. Turners should practice without jumpers until they learn to turn rhythmically.

After your students have learned to turn the rope, they will be ready to jump rope. The following sequence of jumping activities is intended to allow a student to acquire jumping skills progressively.

Step 1. Jump a swaying rope (one that swings back and forth) both "flat footed" and with a "stepping" motion. The jumper takes his position and the motion of the rope begins.

Step 2. Jump a turning rope. Start "inside" and jump as the rope is turned a full circle. Jump with one, both, or alternate feet.

Step 3. Run through without jumping. When the rope (which is being turned toward the jumper—"front doors") is at its highest point, the jumper runs under it and out.

Step 4. Run in, jump once, and run out (front door). Gradually build up to six consecutive jumps.

Step 5. Repeat steps 3 and 4 through the "back doors" (when the rope is being turned away from the jumper).

While part of the class is practicing long jump rope, let some of the children learn to jump alone using a short rope.

Variations

Jumping chants add interest.

> House for sale,
> Inquire within,
> When I move out,
> Let (name) move in.

> Hippity, Hippity, Hop.
> How many times before I stop?
> 1—2—3—4—5— (until jumper misses,
> or use limited number of jumps).

Jump rope relay is played with teams. Each team uses one jump rope. First player jumps rope to a marked line and back again. He then passes the rope to the next teammate. The team finishing first wins.

Elementary Physical Education
The Miniature Olympics
HARRY OXFORD

Elementary Physical Education is definitely being recognized. However, it is still greatly in need of a strong stimulant. Our ideas must be shared and expressed through some type of media, such as a magazine, newspaper or even a national committee. It is my feeling that while the mind of young children are being taught to read and write, they should also be introduced to a good, sound, physical education program, one which is not sporatic in presence, but firmly situated in every elementary school.

My present situation is quite unique in that physical education classes meet twice daily, five days a week with each class being one half hour in length. The program, which I devised, has been adopted by the Wheeling Country Day School. I would like to share parts of my program with other physical education teachers on the elementary school level.

Miniature Olympics

Every year we hold a miniature Olympic Games. The competitors are boys in the first, second, and third grades. They compete within their own grade level. Each boy in the first and second grades competes individually and is allowed to enter three events only. No more than five or six boys are allowed in any one event. You may find that some boys will not place in any event, therefore, its a good practice to keep a list of these boys and put them in an event of just four boys. That way, each boy will win at least one ribbon, as we have ribbons for the first four places.

The third grade competes individually, but they also represent a country. There are three or four boys representing a country of their choice. In addition to competing, the boys are required to look up the history of the Olympics, acquire pertinent facts, and some information concerning the country they represent. These are all read aloud by the author on our first rainy day and then posted on our physical education bulletin board. This research, or intellectual approach, seems to work very well, as it is a tremendous boost to the boy who does well in the classroom but is not particularly proficient in athletic skills. All these short essay papers are required before the Olympics begin.

During a regular Olympic year, boys are assigned as reporters. They are responsible for bringing in clippings from the papers or magazines. At the beginning of each period, they give a short two or three minute talk about the material. The information is also posted on our physical education bulletin board.

Each class has a certain number of activities. We hold two or three activities each period. The boys who are not participating cheer from the side as spectators. They are also assigned various officiating duties. All boys sign up for three activities that they would like to enter. Three events are open to everyone. Three activities are held back so those boys (those not placing in the activities) can enter in an event they are certain to place in; or, only four boys are put in an event.

At the conclusion of the Olympics, we present the ribbons, which are made by the boys during their art period. Our school colors are green and white so the neck ribbons are green and white. The medal discs are gold (1st), silver (2nd), green (3rd), and white (4th). Heavy gold and silver decorator paper is used for the first two medals and green and white railroad board is used for the last two. The writing on the discs is around the edge and reads, "Beauvoir (your school) Olympics" with the year in the center. The ribbon is long enough to be placed over the boy's head.

The medals are presented before the boys leave for Thanksgiving holidays, which leaves about three weeks for the games to take place. The three weeks will permit you plenty of time to cover the events, reporting, and keeping the bulletin board up to date. Each boy's name appears on the bulletin board.

FIRST GRADE

Fifty yard dash
Half lap race
One lap race
Sit-ups
Pull-ups
Throw 6" ball

Punt - volleyball
Obstacle course
Crab race
Rope climb
Standing broad jump

SECOND GRADE

Fifty yard dash
Half lap race
One lap race
Two lap race
Sit-ups
Push-ups
Pull-ups
Basket shooting

Broad jump
High jump
Obstacle course
Throw-football
Punt-football
Rope climb
Crab race
Standing broad jump

THIRD GRADE

Fifty yard dash
Half lap race
One lap race
Two lap race
Sit-ups
Push-ups
Pull-ups
Basket shooting
Broad jump

High jump
Obstacle course
Throw-football
Punt-football
Rope climb
Crab race
Standing broad jump
Field goals
Wrestling

In general, this is a very appealing activity. We try to include all the teachers and the principal. It requires a little planning the first year, but after that it will require very little time. Why not try it? Good luck.

Weight Training for Elementary School Boys?

WESLEY K. RUFF

One need not inquire into studies conducted by psychologists to observe the fact that boys attain considerable social prestige as a result of proficiency in athletic skills.[1, 6] Likewise, those who possess no skill in athletics are seldom sought after by their peers. Those who are skillful are chosen early for participation in games during recess and those who are not skillful must practice at the sidelines, observe, or wait for the teacher to intervene in the natural process of team selection. Boys who are successful in sports activity are considered "chips off the old block" or "real boys" by the layman.

In our culture it is desirable for boys to be big and to show evidence of good nutrition. This goal is primarily born of parental pride. Mothers tend to take pride in the fact that their boys are heavy, because this reflects good maternal care. Since the entire American culture seems to place considerable value on height, boys who are tall are for some reason given more plus points than boys who are not so tall.[4, 6]

It is desirable to have a boy who can stand up for his rights. While it is true that the American culture does not condone a bully, neither does it condone a coward. The American ideal is to have a boy who can stand up for his rights and if necessary defend them in physical combat. In our culture a boy should be capable of participation in rough-and-tumble activities without complaint; as a matter of fact, he is expected to enjoy body-contact activities. In the last 20 years fighting in general has been condemned in most segments of our culture. In spite of this, no red-blooded American wants his boy to be a coward. On the other hand, most of us hope our boys will stop fighting by the time they are nine.

The lay public is not interested in having children attain any specific physical fitness standard. While the Kraus-Weber test and its highly publicized results have excited some professional people in our field, the lay public still looks to performance in games and swimming, rather than touching the toes with the knees straight, chins, push-ups, sit-ups, etc., as a goal they hope their children might attain. As a matter of fact, many parents complain when their children come home with sore muscles as a result of having been given a physical fitness test.

Cultural Limitations

Our culture limits the activities of all of us in very subtle ways. Boys may play with dolls to the age of four or five, but when they go to school it is not acceptable. Adults do not approve of long, feminine hair arrangements for boys, etc. Somehow boys are expected to learn to throw a ball, bat a ball, catch, run, jump, climb and swim by the time they are nine or ten. Very few elementary schools provide any formal instruction in these sports skills, yet proficiency is expected. This expectation is so specific that a child lacking skill is likely to be ridiculed by his peers, in addition to being excluded from sports activity. This form of social pressure is sorely felt by children and adolescents in our culture and must not be overlooked by adults.[1]

Goals for Elementary School Children Expressed by the Profession

An examination of the purposes of elementary school physical education as presented in *Physical Education in the Elementary School* published by the California State Department of Education (1951) reveals that the goals of the professional group differ from the goals of the layman, primarily in that it is obvious that the professional group hopes to utilize physical activity as an educational medium, whereas the average layman appreciates the physical-social value of sports participation, but otherwise considers physical activity pretty much of an end in itself.

Current Interest in Weight Training

There has been a gradual increase in the number of people interested in weight training over the last 25 to 30 years. Weight training came to the schools and colleges in much the same way as did many other athletic activities, as a result of student interest. Coaches and physical educators frowned upon its use and it was not until after World War II that professional people in significant numbers came to accept weight training as a legitimate physical education activity.

With this acceptance came the realization of its potential as a supplementary training medium. This realization was most prominently brought to public and professional attention as a result of Parry O'Brien's spectacular achievements in the shot put. Since that time an ever-increasing number of coaches on both high school and college levels have been seeking to utilize weight training as a means of improving the performance of their athletes in other sports.

Because of the change in attitude on the part of the coaches and the availability of facilities in both high schools and colleges, many boys who are not competitors in sports have taken a vigorous interest in weight training as a means of improving their strength and enhancing their physical appearance. This interest in body building, along with the current emphasis on physical fitness, is reaching such proportions that it causes the author to wonder if it does not represent a change of goals on the part of the layman with regard to what he hopes to attain for himself as a result of participation in physical education activities. Many boys no longer seek a position on an interscholastic or intercollegiate team; such boys appear to be satisfied with the evident self-improvement which results from participation in resistance exercise.

There is still some interest on the part of youth in weight-lifting as a competitive sport; however, those who are interested in weight-lifting competition are so few in number that very few colleges have seen any necessity for establishing this activity as a competitive sport. It is not inconceivable that this sport might grow to significant proportions; however, the basic motivation of social recognition is missing at the present time. Until weight-lifting champions are held in the same esteem as champions in other sports, there will be no real clamor for youth to achieve excellence in this activity.

Resistance exercise in many forms is currently being utilized in rehabilitation. At the present time almost every college trainer makes use of weights in an attempt to strengthen post-operative cases as quickly as possible. This is especially true of post-surgery on knees and shoulders. Trainers are not the only ones using weight exercises for these purposes; one need only visit a well equipped physical therapy facility to discover numerous forms of resistance exercise being utilized.

We may say then that weight training came to the schools as a result of student pressure and student interest. It was taken up by coaches as a supplementary training device; it is a legitimate competitive sport; and it has been utilized extensively as a means of physical rehabilitation. While it may represent a change in our cultural attitudes it is evident that weight training is an activity that will have a definite place in the physical education programs of tomorrow's schools.

What Results Can Reasonably Be Expected

The primary reward for participation in heavy resistance exercise is substantial gain in strength. Not only can the individual expect to gain strength, but through careful application of his training he can expect to gain strength in any specific area he chooses. Physiologists may argue for a good many years to come as to just why this change takes place and how gains in strength may be attained most effectively, but the fact will always remain that regulated resistance exercise will cause the individual to gain strength.

Gains in strength are usually accompanied by gains in girth. For the slender boy this may mean, in addition, some gain in weight. These changes are regarded very favorably by adolescent youth; with today's emphasis upon one's physical appearance, many youths are more concerned with changes in their physical appearance than they are with attainment of additional strength. This fact has brought considerable criticism of the use of weight training—no attempt will be made here to evaluate this except to say that it is consistent with current cultural values and is related to the attainment of a masculine physique. If judgment is to be passed upon the desirability or undesirability of this practice, the judgment must also be passed upon many other facets of our current cultural values.

It is logical to expect some gains in speed; however, these gains will be limited by the extent to which speed is dependent upon strength. It is reasonable to assume that a strong man can lift a heavy object more rapidly than a man who is weak.[3] It is also likely that a man who can climb the rope reasonably well could climb it faster if he were stronger. However, this speed factor is definitely limited by one's inherent neuromuscular physiology—to say this another way, there is no doubt that every man has speed limitations which cannot be surpassed merely by becoming stronger.

No basic neuromuscular reaction-time changes can really be expected as a result of weight training.[5] As stated above, changes in one's speed that are dependent upon nerve stimulation cannot reasonably be expected of weight training. To clarify this point, perhaps an example may be advantageous. If a man were to train in an attempt to attain his optimum speed in moving his foot from the throttle to the brake of a mock automobile, then train vigorously with weights, it would not seem likely that the weight training would improve his reaction time.[8]

No skills other than weight-lifting skills can be expected to improve; for example, if a boy cannot swim well because he lacks skill in swimming, it is not expected that his skill in swimming will improve as a result of lifting weights.

No increase in inherent neuromuscular coordination could be expected. It would surely seem unreasonable to expect that weight training would speed up an individual's ability to learn physical skills not dependent upon strength. Naturally if a skill required considerable strength, there would be some reason to assume that weight training would enhance learning such a skill. It is therefore logical to assume that there are three basic benefits one might reasonably expect as a result of lifting weights: gains in strength; gains in speed to the extent that strength is a factor in speed; and changes in physical appearance resulting from changes in girth. To expect more of weight training is unreasonable and may ultimately be detrimental to this form of physical training.

It may be worthwhile to mention that no evidence has been submitted as a result of authoritative research which would indicate that the use of weight training is harmful or detrimental to one's health or physical performance.[6, 7]

Are Elementary School Children Interested?

Because no studies have been published in this area, observations will of necessity have to be presented. The author has served on the staff of a "coaching camp" for elementary school children and has had considerable opportunity to observe boys who have an opportunity to exercise with weights. As a part of the "camp" program the boys are given a lecture-demonstration on weight-lifting and weight training. Later the boys have an opportunity to explore the weight-lifting room. As a part of the exploration they like to test their strength, however, none of them care to exercise. If left alone they will test themselves with enthusiasm, but within ten minutes they are playing a game elsewhere.

Junior High School boys will occasionally exercise with weights, but they will not exercise with any regularity unless supervised and actually regimented by an older boy or an adult.

Obviously the interests boys have are determined by their total environment. At the present time our culture does not particularly value strength for strength's sake, nor do we favor, for the time being at least, regimentation.

Children are interested in performance skill in games that are played by their peers. This is their source of status. It is difficult to help elementary school children to practice skills in order to attain a better performance in a game. Likewise it is difficult for children to see the relationship of strength to their proficiency in sports, and even more difficult to get them to do regular exercises to increase strength. They want to play.

Appropriate Activity for Elementary School Children?

It would seem obvious in the light of the foregoing discussion that if any effort is to be undertaken to develop an organized physical education program at the elementary level, that program should first aspire to teach a wide variety of sports skills. To increase a child's strength without attention to skill will not provide the social recognition most boys seek, and for this reason alone would probably not attract or hold their interest.

The prime factor in stimulating interest in weight training in schools and colleges has been to improve performance at the top levels of competition. With competition rather carefully controlled, if tolerated at all, on the elementary level, it seems a misspent effort to strive to improve performance of unskilled children by using a means utilized as a supplementary training device by some *skillful* performers. It would seem a far more productive effort to work on improving technique at this age, rather than to concentrate on increasing strength.

In the event that an elementary school were fully staffed with physical educators, and if a well-rounded program were offered, it is conceivable that weight training could be utilized for some underdeveloped children, handicapped children, and possibly selected convalescent cases. Since very few elementary schools offer complete physical education programs and because current interests and *needs* lie in other areas the author concludes that weight training as such is *not* an appropriate organized physical education activity for elementary school boys.

BIBLIOGRAPHY

1. Corey, Stephen M. "The Developmental Tasks of Youth." John Dewey Society, Hollis L. Caswell, ed. *The American High School.* Eighth Year book. New York, Harper & Bros., 1946, p. 70-99.
2. Educational Policies Commission. *School Athletics Problems & Policies.* Washington, D.C., N.E.A., 1914.
3. Endres, John P. "The Effect of Weight Training Exercises Upon the Speed of Muscular Movement." Unpublished Masters Thesis, University of Wisconsin, 1953.
4. Jones, Harold E. "Physical Ability as a Factor in Adjustment in Adolescence." *Journal of Educational Research,* 40:287-301, December 1946.
5. Sperry, R. W. "Action Current Study in Movement Coordination." *Journal General Psychology,* 20:295-313, 1939.
6. Tryon, Caroline M. *Evaluations of Adolescent Personality by Adolescents.* Monographs of the Society of Research in Child Development, Vol. IV, No. 4, Serial No. 23, Washington, D.C., The Society, 1939.
7. Wilkins, B. M. "The Effect of Weight Training on Speed of Movement," *Research Quarterly* 22:361-369, 1952.
8. Zorbas, W. S. & Karpovich, P. V. "The Effect of Weight Lifting Upon the Speed of Muscular Contractions." *Research Quarterly* 22:145-148, 1951.

CHAPTER V

PHYSICAL EDUCATION FOR THE ATYPICAL CHILD

Teaching Motor Skills to the Mentally Retarded
PAUL DUNHAM, JR.

While motor ability is significantly important to the normal child, it is of paramount significance to the mentally retarded child. Benton (1964) states that a genius can afford to be a "motor moron," but a person with an IQ score of 50 cannot. The retarded person's ability to perform motor skills may well determine whether he will attain a reasonable degree of social competence. For this reason, assessment of motor capacity should be an aspect of psychological evaluation for prediction, identification, guidance, and training.

Beck (1956) has pointed out that for the mentally retarded in the primary grades, the special education teacher carries on the physical education instruction; during the intermediate years, the physical education instructor plays a significant role, and finally takes complete charge of students 14 years and older. Thus, it would seem important for physical education and classroom teachers as well as special education personnel to be aware of the information available concerning the development of motor skills in the mentally retarded.

Considerable information has been collected concerning the learning of motor abilities of the mentally retarded. In the absence of experimental studies, however, past experience based on observation of experts should be employed until basic research is conducted. The following techniques should be useful to the beginning teacher for instructing the mentally retarded in the area of motor skills.

Reward
Reward mentally retarded students when they successfully accomplish what they were asked to do. Instructors have employed food, candies, small toys, and social rewards such as hugs, pats, and verbal praise.

Verbal praise has been shown to produce significantly better performance in a group of mentally retarded subjects than in a control group. Ellis and Distefano (1959); Gordon, O'Connor, and Tizard (1955); and O'Connor and Claridge (1955) demonstrated that setting goals for the subject and providing praise and encouragement result in heightened performance and continued improvement. McManis (1965) found that accuracy rank order was the same for normal and retarded subjects under incentive conditions of competition, praise, reproval, and neutrality, in descending order. For the mentally retarded, only competition or praise resulted in significantly better performance.

Verbal praise may affect mentally retarded subjects in different ways. Zigler (1963) found that there was a significant difference in the length of time institutionalized and noninstitutionalized persons played a simple motor skill game. The noninstitutionalized mentally retarded played about as long under both reinforcement conditions, while noninstitutionalized normal subjects played longer under the nonsupport condition. Parsons and Stewart (1966) gave subjects disinterested, impersonal, irrelevant information gathering interviews, and found that they improved at a significantly lower rate over three successive administrations of the Stein-Gestalt test than subjects given warm, supportive, anxiety reducing interviews.

Punishment

Administer punishment sparingly and when warranted, making sure the punishment follows the act immediately. If not punished at once, the mentally retarded child will not associate the punishment with his act but may interpret it as hostility.

Expectations

Expect the mentally retarded child to perform below normal initially, but to improve greatly with practice. Most investigations have found that the mentally retarded are generally inferior to normal children in initial motor skills performance. Reynolds and Stacey (1955) indicated that mentally retarded children were capable of vast improvements of performance on mirror drawing. Baumeister, Hawkins, and Holland (1966) reported that 48 normal subjects had initially superior performance on the pursuit rotor, but with practice the mentally retarded subjects overtook them. Cantor and Stacey (1951) found that on both the Purdue Pegboard and Oseretsky Tests of Motor Proficiency, the adult retarded subjects were generally significantly below the adult norms. Johnson and Blake (1963) gave mentally retarded and normal school children (matched on mental ages) a simple card sorting task and found the retarded subjects to be superior. The same results were obtained on a simple puzzle assembly task. They concluded that in such simple tasks, the older retarded children had an advantage over the younger normal children. Denny (1964), after reviewing the literature, stated that when mentally retarded children are matched with normals on chronological age, the retarded do very poorly at the outset on motor skills, but with continued practice show a rapid improvement, and if the task is not too difficult may even catch up. Francis and Rarick (1959) gave a battery of 11 motor performance tests designed to measure strength, balance, and agility of 284 mentally retarded children. Their performance was compared with that of normal children. The results indicated that the retarded children were markedly inferior to the normal children. The relationship between measures of intelligence and motor performance were similar to correlations obtained between these variables on normal subjects. The authors pointed out that the basic factors underlying the causes of the motor retardation must await further investigation.

The fact that mentally retarded children initially perform below normal on motor skills seems well established through research studies. The important aspect of this consideration for educators, however, is not the initial lack of skill but rather the learning potential. There seems to be substantial evidence in the studies cited to support the thesis that with practice the mentally retarded can be expected to exhibit considerable improvement. Francis and Rarick (1959) in discussion of their findings noted that the unusually high performance peaks obtained by some individuals suggests that a higher level of performance is attainable by the slow learner.

Type of Practice Sessions

Short, frequent practice sessions usually prove to be more effective than distribution of practice sessions. Boldt (1953), comparing 60 retarded subjects and 60 college students on a block turning task, found that the retarded subjects improved more and faster than the college students under distributive as compared to massed practice.

It would seem advisable for teachers of motor skills to employ a distributed type of practice for the mentally retarded, mindful of each individual's attention span, performance, and motivation. Material should be prepared to allow for numerous and varied presentations of the subject matter.

Reminiscence and Retention

Mentally retarded subjects frequently exhibit reminiscence and retention. Reminiscence can be defined as the improvement from the last trial of the previous session to the first trial of the following session—that is, improvement without practice. Retention is the retaining of a particular level of skill from one testing to another. Warm up is the rapid increase in performance level during a specific period of time. All are of interest to the teacher of motor skills, but particularly warm up. Instruction has little value if the learner has no capacity to retain what he has learned.

Baumeister, Hawkins, and Holland (1966) found that retarded subjects exhibited a comparable amount of reminiscence to normals. They also found more warm up in retarded than in normal children. Barnett and Cantor (1957) found more reminiscence following massed practice as opposed to distributive practice. Ellis, Pryer, and Barnett (1960) observed retention and reminiscence in both normal and retarded subjects, but found that normal children had more retention and warm up than the retarded children. Denny (1964), Gordon, O'Connor, and Tizard (1955) and Tizard and Loos (1954) have all observed retention in retarded subjects' performance on motor skills.

Goals with Incentives

Realistic goals should be supported by proper incentive of the subject and instructor so that motor skill proficiency can develop gradually and systematically. Numerous investigators—Gordon, O'Connor, and Tizard (1955); O'Connor and Claridge (1955); and Ellis and Distefano (1959)—have demonstrated that setting goals for the subjects and providing praise and encouragement result in heightened performance and continued improvement. In a similar investigation, Heber (1959) found that subjects performing under a highly preferred incentive condition did significantly better than the subjects performing under a less preferred incentive condition. Results also indicated that the more able mentally retarded children could respond differently to incentive variation. Denny (1964) stated that motivating retarded children is necessary in order to build what they had not learned incidentally during their early years. Cantor (1960) found that competing with members of the opposite sex did not interfere with performance of the subjects.

Individual Attention

The more severely retarded children need more individual attention. Ellis, Pryer, Distefano, and Pryer (1960) and Ellis, Pryer, and Barnett (1960) found that maze learning was substantially related to test intelligence. Sloan (1951) stated that as tasks on the Oseretsky Test of Motor Proficiency become more complex, a greater relationship with IQ level appears. Cantor and Stacey (1951) stated that the more operations involved in the Purdue Pegboard task, the more the adult retarded individuals deviate from established norms. Malpass's (1960) results suggested that the motor proficiency of retarded children is more highly related to intellectual ability than it is in normal children.

Ellis (1963) stated that individuals in the lower IQ ranges do not demonstrate as much coordination, precision, and speed of reaction as normal persons do. On the other hand, many visitors to classes for the educable mentally retarded children are surprised at the motor proficiency of many of these students. While few studies of the severely retarded are available, direct observation of their motor performance indicates considerable limitation in their motor proficiency.

The teacher of motor skills should keep in mind that even though there is considerable evidence indicating that the moderately retarded child's initial level of motor performance is not as high as that of the normal child, studies by Sloan (1951), Francis and Rarick (1959), and Malpass (1960) have not demonstrated that retarded students have less capacity to learn motor skills.

Socialization

In advanced stages of learning, the retarded student can profit from socializing. Abel (1938), employing a pencil maze test to study the influence of "social facilitation" on motor performance, found that the retarded subjects profited more from working in pairs rather than alone.

Smith and Hurst (1961) obtained results that supported the hypothesis that motor ability (as defined by the Lincoln-Oseretsky Scale) plays a significant role in peer acceptance. Social status was defined in the study as the number of peer contests a child initiated or received.

These studies seem to indicate that the retarded student might well profit and show performance improvement from learning situations in which he participates closely with other students. These associations need not necessarily be other retarded students, for Johnson (1963) pointed out, after reviewing the literature concerning special education, that:

> There is almost universal agreement that mentally handicapped children enrolled in special classes achieve, academically, significantly less than similar children who remain in regular grades. In the area of motor or manual skills, there appears to be no difference in their development (p. 66).

Johnson contended that the solution is not the removal or restriction of pressure on the mentally handicapped child, but rather the establishment of learning activities that are meaningful and have purpose and value. He believes that realistic stress should be introduced so that the child will have the drive or motivation to learn, and the demands of performance should be at a level at which the child can achieve with application of some effort. Johnson suggested that teachers should adopt a positive rather than negative attitude, concentrating on individual abilities rather than on individual limitations.

Competition and Motivation

Competition and motivation can assist the retarded in acquisition of motor skills.

Hunt (1955) observed that the retarded express a desire for competition and usually express desire for social praise, but frequently do not respond to competition very well, often becoming discouraged and aggressive when they lose.

Stevenson and Snyder (1960) obtained evidence that the effect of a particular incentive condition is influenced significantly by the condition that preceded it. In a later study, Kass and Stevenson (1961) found that retarded children had more trouble learning a discrimination task after a failure experience than they had after a success experience. Zigler, Hodgden, and Stevenson (1958) found that mentally retarded subjects spent longer periods of time performing simple motor tasks than normal subjects under both support and nonsupport conditions. Cantor (1960), as previously noted, found that performance was not interfered with by competing with members of the opposite sex.

Suggested Actions

In situations in which experimental research is either lacking or not applicable, past experience is most helpful to those teaching motor skills to the mentally retarded. The author through experience has found the following actions, cautions, and principles to be invaluable.

1. Use the same tone of voice each time you speak to the student. Your voice may well be his major clue to your feelings toward him.
2. Use the same gestures, for the same reason as above, noting also that these procedures will present a consistency that will reduce the likelihood of the student's becoming confused.
3. Be firm. Make sure students do what you say.
4. Use the same words each time in reinforcing the student. He may have considerable difficulty understanding you.
5. Reward the student while he is still performing the desired act; he may not otherwise associate his reward with the action performed. However, put a delay between an undesirable act of behavior and a situation for which you

plan to reward him. For instance, a boy hits another student, you tell him to stop and he does so; if you immediately reward him, he might well have difficulty separating the two distinct acts and view them as a whole. Thus, you have unintentionally reinforced his hitting another boy.

6. Watch off guard actions. Much of your teaching will be informal and may well communicate unintended attitudes or feelings.
7. Share and discuss your progress and procedures with other teachers, benefitting from their past experience.
8. Be patient! Teach simple, easy tasks first, gradually moving on to the more difficult as the students' performances dictate. Progress is sometimes very slow.
9. Keep complete and accurate records. Good records facilitate progress, show improvement, and can be used to justify the program.

Fundamental Principles

In teaching motor skills to the mentally retarded, there are some basic fundamentals which are essential and beneficial:

1. Evaluate the mentally retarded student carefully and attempt to learn as much as possible before training begins. Establish the student's present level of skill and readiness to learn.
2. Keep learning situations pleasant; the mentally retarded learn much faster when their efforts lead to enjoyable activity.
3. Repetition, practice, and imitation are necessary.
4. Use play situations in place of drill when possible.
5. Employ equipment in a manner that is profitable to individuals specifically.
6. Be versatile and ready for anything. Have a variety of activities available for implementation, and be able to present each a number of different ways.
7. Be sensitive to students' needs, desires, and safety. They are more dependent upon you than normal children would be under similar circumstances.
8. Be involved with each student, not in the emotional sense, but in the sense that you are completely and totally dedicated to his growth, improvement, and well being.

REFERENCES

Abel, T. The influence of social facilitation on motor performance at different levels of intelligence. *American Journal of Psychology,* 1938, 51, 379-389.

Barnett, C. D., and Canton, C. N. Pursuit rotor performance in mental defectives as a function of distribution of practice. *Perceptual Motor Skills,* 1957, 7, 191-197.

Baumeister, A. A., Hawkins, W. and Holland, J. Motor learning and knowledge of results. *American Journal of Mental Deficiency,* 1966, 70, 590-594.

Beck, H. S. Present status of physical education of special classes for the educable mentally handicapped. *American Journal of Mental Deficiency,* 1956, 51, 117-120.

Benton, A. Psychological evaluation and differential diagnosis in mental retardation. In H. A. Stevens & R. Heger (Eds.), *Mental retardation: A review of research.* Chicago: University of Chicago Press, 1964.

Boldt, R. F. Motor learning in college students and mental defectives. In F. G. Brooks (Ed.), *Proceedings of Iowa Academy of Science.* Des Moines: State of Iowa, 1953, 60, 500-505.

Cantor, N. Motor performance of defectives as a function of competition with same- and opposite-sex opponents. *American Journal of Mental Deficiency,* 1960, 65, 358-362.

Cantor, G. N., and Stacey, C. L. Manipulative dexterity in mental defectives. *American Journal of Mental Deficiency,* 1951, 56, 401-410.

Denny, M. Research in learning and performance. In H. A. Stevens and R. Heber (Eds.), *Mental retardation: A review of research.* Chicago: University of Chicago Press, 1964.

Ellis, N. R. *Handbook of mental deficiency: Psychological theory and research.* New York: McGraw-Hill, 1963.

Ellis, N. R., and Distefano, J., Jr. Effects of verbal urging and praise upon rotary pursuit performance in mental defectives. *American Journal of Mental Deficiency,* 1959, 64, 486-490.

Ellis, N. S., Pryer, M., and Barnett, C. Motor learning and retention in normals and defectives. *Perceptual and Motor Skills,* 1960, 10, 83-91.

Ellis, N. R., Pryer, M. W., Distefano, M. K., and Pryer, R. S. Learning in mentally defective, normal, and superior subjects. *American Journal of Mental Deficiency,* 1960, 64, 725-734.

Francis, R. J., and Rarick, G. L. Motor characteristics of the mentally retarded. *American Journal of Mental Deficiency,* 1959, 63, 792-811.

Gordon, S., O'Connor, N., and Tizard, J. Some effects of incentives on the performance of imbeciles on a repetitive task. *American Journal of Mental Deficiency,* 1955, 60, 371-377.

Heber, R. Motor task performance of high grade mentally retarded males as a function of magnitude of incentive. *American Journal of Mental Deficiency,* 1959, 63, 667-671.

Hunt, V. *Recreation for the handicapped.* Englewood Cliffs, N.J.: Prentice-Hall, 1955.

Johnson, G. Special education for the mentally handicapped—a paradox. *Exceptional Children,* 1963, 29, 62-69.

Johnson, G., and Blake, K. A. *Learning performance of retarded and normal children.* Syracuse: Syracuse University Press, 1963.

Kass, N., and Stevenson, H. W. The effect of pretraining reinforcement conditions on learning by normal and retarded children. *American Journal of Mental Deficiency,* 1961, 66, 76-80.

Malpass, L. F. Motor proficiency in institutionalized and noninstitutionalized retarded children and normal children. *American Journal of Mental Deficiency,* 1960, 64, 1012-1015.

McManis, D. L. Pursuit-rotor performance of normal and retarded children in four verbal-incentive conditions. *Child Development,* 1965, 36, 667-683.

O'Connor, N., and Claridge, G. S. The effect of goal setting and encouragement on the performance of imbecile men. *Quarterly Journal of Experimental Psychology,* 1955, 7, 37-45.

Parsons, O. A., and Stewart, K. D. Effects of supportive versus disinterested interviews on perceptual-motor performance in brain-damaged and neurotic patients. *Journal of Consulting Psychology,* 1966, 30, 260-266.

Reynolds, W. F., and Stacey, C. L. A comparison of normals and subnormals in mirror drawing. *Journal of Genetic Psychology,* 1955, 87, 301-308.

Sloan, W. Motor proficiency and intelligence. *American Journal of Mental Deficiency,* 1951, 55, 394-406.

Smith, J. R., and Hurst, J. G. The relationship of motor abilities and peer acceptance of mentally retarded children. *American Journal of Mental Deficiency,* 1961, 66, 81-85.

Stevenson, H. W., and Snyder, L. C. Performance as a function of the interaction of incentive conditions. *Journal of Personality,* 1960, 28, 1-11.

Tizard, J., and Loos, F. M. The learning of a spatial relations test by adult imbeciles. *American Journal of Mental Deficiency,* 1954, 59, 85-90.

Zigler, E. Rigidity and social reinforcement effects in the performance of institutionalized and non-institutionalized normal and retarded children. *Journal of Personality,* 1963, 31, 258-269.

Zigler, E. F., Hodgen, L., and Stevenson, H. W. The effect of support and non-support on the performance of normal and feeble minded children. *Journal of Personality,* 1958, 26, 106-122.

Some Psychological Factors In Motivating Handicapped Students In Adapted Physical Education

JOHN R. SCHOON

It is accepted that physical education, adapted to the individual's capacity, is of great potential benefit to the student physically, psychologically, and socially. It is assumed that the physical education instructor is a person with adequate preparation and experience. Creating a wholesome classroom climate, establishing student-teacher rapport, directing the student into worthwhile activities, teaching proper attitudes, and working with the student toward realistic goals all take on new importance when the handicapped are involved. Today, after centuries of abuse, neglect, and misunderstanding, handicapped children are finally realizing opportunities rightfully theirs.

Innumerable labels have been bestowed upon the word, "handicap." It has been stated that a condition depends upon the situation and its demands to determine whether or not it is a handicap (14:9). Such a view might be acceptable from certain standpoints, i.e., job opportunities, social situations, and family living, but it implies that no infant is handicapped, because no demands are made on it, and no one is handicapped while he is asleep, for the same reason. Notwithstanding all efforts to define the term, "handicap" will refer to a person with a difference that restricts him competitively (7:48). Occasionally it is used synonomously with the more obvious and medically recognized, "disability."

A handicap was formerly considered detrimental to a citizen's effective participation in society. Handicaps were said to be the cause of serious maladjustments: virtually all handicapped persons had problems of maladjustment brought about by their handicaps. Frequently, efforts of genius were cited as compensation resulting from a handicap. How convenient were those explanations of any behavior which deviated from "normal." Such views are today regarded as gross miscalculations. We know that increasing numbers of handicapped persons are well-adjusted and capable of being genuinely interested in various fields of endeavor for primary satisfaction derived therefrom and not for compensatory rewards (14:118). It is true, however, that unpleasant experiences accompanying an illness can make a child more vulnerable to the effects of that illness (6:11). One of the aims of adapted physical education is to assist the student in coping with his condition and asserting a fuller command of his situation.

Inasmuch as the handicapped person is often shy, somewhat withdrawn, and reluctant to try something new, the instructor in adapted physical education uses special means to elicit participation in the activity program. (It is assumed that a student capable of attending school can engage in some activity.) If possible, the student should begin with some activity in which he is already interested and from which he gains immediate satisfaction. He will benefit from the enjoyment derived from such "interest" activity, and the mental "lift" will help prepare him for a more strenuous exercise routine, if such a routine is prescribed.

Group Activity

Activities which give immediate satisfaction often involve only mild exercise but also include those requiring considerable energy output. The latter are indicated for those handicapped by blindness or partial blindness and others who have learned cautious movement or lived an almost completely sedentary existence. This is their opportunity to release tension through vigorous activity in an appropriately friendly, permissive, and safe environment. This is also their opportunity to benefit from social interactions found in a group situation, which will enhance their effectiveness in social encounters.

An added advantage of having a sizeable group in adapted physical education is that nearly every handicapped person benefits from associating with other handicapped people. They are stimulated by seeing others cope with their handicaps. Frequently, one considers himself more fortunate than another who is less handicapped, because of the kind of disability. Thus, inspiration is gained in various and sometimes inexplicable ways.

Much of the activity in this program will not render an immediate reward but will yield more of an intermediate satisfaction. Consequently, motivation becomes more difficult. It becomes necessary to appeal to the student's sense of values; this is certain to involve his self concept—or body image. This approach can be made only after satisfactory student-teacher rapport has been established, the student has become more familiar with the physical surroundings and decided that this class experience is nothing to fear, and some goal has been determined. What does the experience promise?

Greater independence can be achieved by a handicapped individual through physical education activities. The student with lower extremity involvement can embark upon a program of progressive resistance exercises to strengthen his upper body. Stronger upper extremities enable him to move about more on his own and with less dependence on others' help. New freedom achieved through added strength is not lightly regarded. Concomitantly, the student realizes greater self-esteem, greater self-reliance, and a feeling of increased security. The promise of security appeals to those of all ages.

The instructor may appeal to the student's desire to get along better with others. The epileptic improves his handling of inter-personal relationships by participating in the group activities of an adapted physical education class. Through this participation, at first reluctant, he conquers the dread that formerly precluded social interaction. The teenage epileptic also benefits from age-mate contacts, heretofore unknown, available in coeducational phases of the program. Hence, self-confidence in social situations is attained.

Through the interaction of the program, *the student has an opportunity to acquire desirable attitudes concerning his handicap.* If he is easily irritated by public reactions to his disability he must learn that it is *he* who sets the mood. The instructor assists in teaching him about his condition, its implications, and prognosis, and aids in his acquistion of a realistic and calm outlook which will benefit him in his social intercourse.

The teacher may often appeal to the student's desire to be attractive to others; this is applicable to the obese individual. If his desire is sincere and sufficiently intense, the student will be willing to discipline himself regarding diet and exercise in order to achieve a slimmer profile and enjoy greater acceptance rather than attract ridicule because of unseemly adiposity.

Through activity planned for increased strengthening of the entire body *the student's faculties can improve to enable greater scholastic achievement;* this also involves alternating periods of stress and relaxation. Scholastic achievement is highly prized by most young people, especially those of the upper and middle economic strata of society (9:220).

Working with a person whose handicap has been acquired after the development of some or all of his ideas about himself is more difficult than working with one who has never had to make changes or adjustments in his self concept (2:42). It is hard to determine how long the injured person will cling to his past—to the "golden age" when his body was whole, or relatively so. Perhaps upon his entrance to class he is "ripe for plucking"—that is, ready to emerge from a depressed, sedentary mood, and will respond to the open challenge presented by the opportunities of class routine. It could be that all he needs at this point is an invitation to "get into the swing of things." It seems that our cultural background would assist the instructor at this point, for our heritage has been a dynamic one, and, as a people, we have never turned our back to the challenge of competition.

Motivating the student through the use of distant rewards or remote satisfaction is most difficult. The promise of continued health to a young diabetic "if she sticks to the rules" of regulated diet, exercise, rest, and insulin will hardly affect her behavior. A "small error" in judgment—the kind most of us commit frequently—would prove a major disaster to her. The role of the teacher in this instance is that of a constant friend and willing listener; the teacher must be a willing listener all the time, anyway, in order to help people rather than cases. The need for a listener is not uncommon but it is one that must be fulfilled perfectly or not at all.

People whose injuries have involved disfigurement of one kind or another often learn just what the important things are in this life. With this individual the self-concept cannot be built upon an improved appearance but it can be enhanced by emphasizing the importance of life's nobler virtues—kindness, love, hope, prudence, faith, justice, etc. Youngsters have proved receptive to this approach, for Roth states that he has repeatedly observed in teenagers a zest for life and useful service to others (10:283).

Years ago, Cabot set forth *four things which men live by—work, play, love, worship.* No one is disabled to the extent that prohibits all appreciation of these things (4:16). Because of this truth *the instructor of adapted physical education attempts to reveal the student's potential and assist in its development.* An effort to encourage excellence in a field of endeavor helps diminish the possibility of an inferiority complex (14:83). Personal improvement in the physical, social, and psychological realms will ultimately aid the student in later adjustment and employment.

BIBLIOGRAPHY

1. Carlson, Earl R., *Born That Way,* The John Day Company, New York, 1941.
2. Daniels, Arthur S., *Adapted Physical Education,* Harper.
3. Davis, John E., *Principles and Practices of Rehabilitation,* A. S. Barnes and Company, New York, 1943.
4. Garrett, James F., editor, *Psychological Aspects of Physical Disability,* Department of Health, Education, and Welfare, U. S. Government Printing Office, Washington, D.C.
5. Grayson, Morris, *Psychiatric Aspects of Rehabilitation,* The Institute of Physical Medicine and Rehabilitation, New York University, 1952.
6. Hood, Oreste E., *Your Child or Mine; The Brain-Injured Child and His Hope,* Harper and Brothers, Publishers, New York, 1957.
7. Hunt, Valerie, *Recreation for the Handicapped,* Prentice-Hall, Inc., New York, 1955.
8. Jersild, Arthur T., *In Search of Self,* Bureau of Publications, Teachers College, Columbia University, New York, 1952.
9. Morse, William C., and Wingo, G. Max, *Psychology and Teaching,* Scott, Foresman and Company, Chicago, 1955.
10. Roth, Arthur, *The Teen-Age Years,* Doubleday and Company, Inc., Garden City, New York, 1960.
11. Schilder, Paul, *The Image and Appearance of the Human Body,* International Universities Press, Inc., New York, 1950.
12. Stafford, George T., and Kelly, Ellen D., *Preventive and Corrective Physical Education,* Third Edition, The Ronald Press Company, New York, 1958.
13. Wallin, J. E. Wallace, *Children With Mental and Physical Handicaps,* Prentice-Hall, Inc., New York, 1949.
14. Wright, Beatrice A., *Physical Disability—A Psychological Approach,* Harper and Brothers, Publishers, New York, 1960.

Social Groupings Enhance Recreation Opportunities for Retarded Children

VERN H. MCGRIFF

There are advantages of both segregated and purposefully integrated social groupings for recreation for mildly retarded children and slow learners. Schools can assume a leadership role in assisting these children to develop essential personal and social values and skills. Such values and skills will not only contribute to the personal satisfaction that these children enjoy now, but also will enable them to enjoy and utilize effectively leisure time later on as part of normal community life.

In a study of opportunities and provision of recreation services for mentally retarded children in a large, metropolitan area, it became evident that public schools are in a vital position to lead the way.[12] Advantages of appropriately combining the use of segregated and integrated social groupings also became apparent. Public schools serve this large group of mildly retarded children and slow learners; therefore, the findings and implications of this study take on added significance for these children who benefit and function satisfactorily in planned integrated groupings under certain circumstances.

Why should there be so much concern about recreation for retarded children? It is estimated that only about five percent of the mentally retarded population can be found in institutions.[8] The other 95 percent, then, are living at home. Families and communities are faced with many hardships in attempting to make possible a full life for these children who spend many idle hours at home and in the community. A major problem for them is to develop social competence and to use leisure time effectively.[14]

Universal needs of man do not change simply because a person's mental or physical efficiency differs from the norm; therefore, retarded children have the same basic needs as nonretarded children. Recreation—viewed as an important right and need for all persons —takes on added significance for retarded children since they have limited social outlets or involvements. They often lack skills, necessary guidance, public interest, and public acceptance. Retarded persons need to belong, to create, and to feel secure and significant.[4]

Community recreation programs for retarded children offer varied activities and services. In many communities, however, where organized recreation facilities are available, they are seldom used by retarded persons.[11] What are they doing with their leisure time? One institution, which received a grant to study the problem of its returnees, reported that 52 percent of the mentally retarded returnees came back because of their inability to handle leisure time —not because of difficulty adjusting to their employment situation.[2]

Studies have been done on the occupational adjustments of retarded adults. These studies have indicated that main reasons for job failures were often for reasons other than ability. They included temperamental instability involving inability to withstand ridicule by fellow employees, inability to assume responsibility and take advice, and unsatisfactory home conditions.[3] [5] [13] [15]

Automation is one of the social forces decreasing the number of unskilled jobs. Since these are the kinds of jobs which are most likely to be filled by retarded individuals, it follows that retarded persons will require more assistance in the future to handle their increased leisure time.[10] Exclusive emphasis on prevocational and vocational training for this group may not really be meeting their present and future needs.

Experimental studies have shown that positive results were obtained when teachers attempted to restore and reinforce in retarded children a growing sense of self-confidence through repeated successful experiences. These children strengthened their personal and social skills in making improved adjustments in the community.[7] Studies have also shown that rhythmic and physical activities are beneficial to retarded children.[9] [16] An experimental study to develop a curriculum for retarded children demonstrated that play activity was a means for teaching more abstract concepts from concrete experiences.[6]

Some of these children exhibit mild intellectual deficits not because of inadequate intelligence but because of the lack of opportunity to experience many perceptions around a variety of events. Recreation programs need to provide a highly stimulating and structured environment if the potential of these children is to be attained. The large group of mildly retarded children and slow learners approach the norm in appearance and in physical traits. With appropriate guidance and emphasis on developing behavioral patterns of responsibility and sociability, they can adapt and lose much of their atypical appearance, mannerisms, and behavior.

It can be seen, then, that schools occupy a significant place in relation to this segment in society. Society can no longer afford to impose a social stigma on these children and force them to become victims of home isolation. When schools recognize that teaching recreation skills is a serious responsibility and make deliberate efforts to provide for this—not leaving it to chance—then positive changes may be identified in the adaptive behavior of these children. Such efforts contribute to their achievement of constructive and socially worthwhile goals, representing one effective way to assist them in developing social competence and using leisure time effectively. How, then, can social groupings of mildly retarded and slow learning children enhance their recreational opportunities?

Segregated Social Groupings

Many advantages of segregated social groupings must be recognized. Participation in segregated activities has improved socialization of retarded children—improved them physically, improved their personal habits, developed their self-confidence, facilitated their adjustment at home, and facilitated self-acceptance and acceptance of other retarded children.[12] In some instances, after physical and social skill development and training of retarded children in segregated groups, some of them were able to become involved on an independent basis with nonretarded children, for example, in street games.

Segregated patterns represent the best type of social grouping for program modifications and adaptations to serve the largest number of retarded children and the youngest age group. Reasons for establishing segregated as opposed to integrated programs include: unacceptable behavior of retarded to nonretarded child, ability to increase variety of activities offered, and ability to serve a larger number of retarded children by including others than just mildly retarded children.

As leaders gain more sophistication in identifying specific strengths and weaknesses among the children, the behavior of some of them may be altered, e.g., increasing their social awareness, minimizing and sometimes eliminating atypical behavior and dress, and assisting them to develop a more wholesome self-concept. Where specific recreational skills are taught in programs clearly identifying and sequencing components of instruction for the retarded children, they are able to succeed in learning a variety of skills by not being forced to make unnecessary conceptual leaps. Segregated groupings for retarded children provide more opportunities for skill instruction and a direct and expedient way of meeting their specific recreation needs.

Integrated Social Groupings

When mildly retarded children are expected to participate in activities with other children on a casual or unplanned basis, the retarded group participates in limited activities. In addition, smaller numbers of them participate. The point becomes clear that these children should not be left to plan for their own activities on an independent basis. Integration is not a fortuitous occurrence.

When integration of mildly retarded children is a planned and deliberately arranged approach, wider varieties of activities in which they participate with nonretarded children are offered. There is a positive effort made to promote the acceptance of retarded children as participants and to involve them in the activities of regular programs. Where modifications or adjustments are needed, these may also be done with minimal effort.

Combining Integrated and
Segregated Groupings

Combinations of social groupings seem to offer the greatest flexibility in providing opportunities for retarded children to participate in recreation activities. Advantages include: (1) having specific times for retarded children to enter into activities on a segregated basis offering a wide variety of activities; (2) planning certain activities on an integrated basis whereby retarded children could participate in the regular program; and (3) making available to retarded children, as well as nonretarded, activities and facilities on an unplanned integrated basis.

Combinations of social groupings provide retarded children with the advantages of segregated groups. At the same time certain experiences are available to them in which they can participate even though with some limitations with nonretarded children. Moreover, by integrating retarded children with nonretarded children, the program introduces the retarded children to a nonretarded society. By doing this in a supervised setting, the likelihood for nonretarded children's acceptance of retarded children is enhanced.

Segregation used in combination with unplanned and planned groupings provides opportunities for retarded children to participate with nonretarded children when feasible. The ultimate objective of combined groupings, then, should be to prepare those retarded children, who are able, to function in integrated settings whenever and wherever this is feasible. The necessity for deliberate planning cannot be overemphasized for effective integration.

In describing integrating services for these children, a recent report indicated that one must determine types of activities common to handicapped and nonhandicapped children that can be used in integrating the two groups; determine conditions and approaches to activities most conducive to integration; and ascertain the values and limitations of integrative and segregative activity.[1] Ways in which mildly retarded children are grouped with nonretarded children to develop the potential in recreation opportunities for the former are highly significant. There are some times when retarded children should be segregated and other times when planned integration is desirable.

The demand by personnel in the fields of physical, health, and recreation education continues for information and assistance with which they may approach and solve problems creating roadblocks to progress in various aspects of programs for exceptional children.

REFERENCES

1. American Association for Health, Physical Education, and Recreation and National Recreation and Park Association. *Physical Education and Recreation for Handicapped Children: A Study Conference on Research and Demonstration Needs* (Washington, D.C.: AAHPER, 1969).
2. Blum, Charles W. "Mental Retardates: Fine Citizens." (Paper read at the Northeastern Conference, American Association on Mental Deficiency, Kiamesha, New York, October 16, 1967).

3. Bobroff, Allen. "Economic Adjustment of 121 Adults Formerly Students in Classes for the Mental Retardates," *American Journal of Mental Deficiency,* LX (January 1956), pp. 525-35.
4. Carlson, Reynold E., and others. *Recreation in American Life* (Belmont, California: Wadsworth Publishing Company, Inc., 1963).
5. Cassidy, Viola M., and Phelps, Harold R. *Postschool Adjustment of Slow Learning Children: A Study of Persons Previously Enrolled in Special Classes in Ohio* (Columbus, Ohio: Ohio State University, 1955).
6. Connor, Frances P., and Talbot, Mabel E. *An Experimental Curriculum for Young Mentally Retarded Children* (New York: Bureau of Publications, Teachers College, Columbia University, 1964).
7. Dayton, Neil A. "The Real Goal in the Education and Training of the Mentally Retarded in Residential Schools," *Mental Retardation,* I (June 1963), pp. 136-37, 182-83.
8. Johnson, G. Orville. "Psychological Characteristics of the Mentally Retarded," in *Psychology of Exceptional Children and Youth.* William M. Cruickshank, ed. (Englewood Cliffs, New Jersey: Prentice-Hall, Inc., 1963).
9. Kelley, Frances P. "Recreational Service for the Retarded—An Urgent Need," *Recreation in Treatment Centers,* III (September 1964), pp. 12-15.
10. Kirk, Samuel A. *Educating Exceptional Children* (Boston: Houghton-Mifflin Company, 1962).
11. Mayo, Leonard W. (chairman). *Report to the President: A Proposed Program for National Action to Combat Mental Retardation* (Washington, D.C.: The President's Panel on Mental Retardation, October 1962).
12. McGriff, Vern H. *Selected Administrative Aspects of Tax-Supported Recreation Programs in Relation to Social Grouping Patterns of Mentally Retarded Children* (Doctoral dissertation, Teachers College, Columbia University, 1968).
13. O'Connor, N. "Defectives Working in the Community," *American Journal of Mental Deficiency,* LIX (October 1954), pp. 173-80.
14. Oettinger, Katherine B. "Opening Doors for the Retarded Child," *The New York Times Magazine* (May 12, 1963).
15. Peckham, Ralf A. "Problems in Job Adjustment of the Mentally Retarded," *American Journal of Mental Deficiency,* LVI (October 1951), pp. 448-53.
16. Stein, Julian U. "The Potential of Physical Activity for the Mentally Retarded Child," *Journal of Health, Physical Education, Recreation,* XXXVII (April 1966), pp. 25-28.

Creativity in Teaching Physical Education to the Physically Handicapped Child

DAGNY CHRISTENSEN

Four days of substituting in a special school for orthopedically handicapped children in the Los Angeles City Schools was one of my most enjoyable and unforgettable teaching experiences. It was enjoyable until time for physical education. I am sure panic was evident on my face, for to me physical education meant games and other vigorous activities.

One boy who sensed my concern said sympathetically, "Don't worry, we'll take care of this period ourselves." A specially trained physical education teacher came periodically—the rest of the time the children were on their own. I watched apprehensively at first and then in admiration as the physical education period progressed. A girl lying on a cot slowly moved her hands to recorded music; two boys in wheel chairs played checkers; others played lap games. Outside a boy shot baskets from his wheel chair; an epileptic boy retrieved the ball, took his shot, and then threw it to the boy in the wheel chair. Everyone was having a fine time.

As I watched, I remembered another time long ago when I overheard a little asthmatic girl say wistfully, "I wish I could take physical education and be able to run just once in my life." That girl was in a public school classroom relegated to watch on the sidelines while her classmates ran, jumped, and shouted their joy of just being alive.

How many other physically handicapped children in other classrooms are similarly relegated? Academically, many are able to be in a regular classroom, but seemingly they are not able to participate in physical education. Creative approaches designed to bring about social, psychological, emotional, and, to a degree, physical success for physically handicapped boys and girls who have been sitting quietly on the sidelines will help relieve frustrations felt by both teachers and children. Physically handicapped children can be included and taught in physical education.

I have a boy afflicted with cerebral palsy in my fifth grade classroom. Mickey has come a long way from the day he entered kindergarten in a wheel chair. He has progressed from the chair, to crutches, to walking with a cane, to walking unassisted in a mannequine-like walk. He has good use of his arms, shoulders, head and neck, and trunk. His attitude toward himself and his peers is good; academic ability is average.

A typical physical education unit program includes soccer-football type activities in the fall, basketball-volleyball-self-testing activities in the winter, and softball-track and field in the spring. Rhythms are taught throughout the year. Mickey should be able to participate in each of these activities and be limited only in degree by his condition. He should do well in any activity involving use of arms, hands, chest, shoulders, trunk, neck, and head. Following are representative adaptations and modifications which enable Mickey to participate in typical unit activities.

Soccer. Practice chest, shoulder, and head blocking and some leg trapping; be a lineman in line soccer, a goalie in three line soccer, and take half the goal in modified soccer.

Football. Practice forward passing and catching from stationary positions; play end man in football end ball.

Basketball. Practice all phases and shots from stationary positions; participate in lead-up games involving passing, catching, and goal shooting.

Volleyball. Work on serving and under-and-over volleys; assign a stationary position in which he serves for his team in lead-up games and activities.

Self-testing activities. Perform leg roll, seal walk, wheel barrow (he is the barrow); hand wrestle; learn grips on the horizontal bar; travel on the horizontal ladder; do some balancing activities with a wand.

Rhythms. Do modified mimetics and any rhythmic activity involving shoulder, head, arm, and trunk movements; use rhythm sticks or other instruments as the rest of the class does dances in which he is unable to participate.

Softball. Practice throwing, catching, fielding, and batting.

Every teacher has favorite lead-up games and low organized activities for each unit; many programs include different units from those discussed. Each teacher will have to modify and adapt activities for his own particular situation. Application of the principles reflected in the activities discussed would be appropriate for any unit.

A creative teacher can devise lead-up games in which the handicapped youngster's particular strengths are stressed. The class itself can invent games in which the handicapped child can participate and contribute.

In physical education, as in other areas of education, emphasis on the individual has become more and more pronounced. One of the exciting trends promoting individual participation at one's own level lies in problem solving activities embodied in movement exploration. Movement exploration holds great promise for physically handicapped children enrolled in regular classrooms. Each child explores different movements he can make at his own level, at his own speed, and in his own way without being pressured by his peers or performance standards. He can experience more physical success than in more structured activities.

The teacher presents a challenge; the child explores independently and discovers for himself where he can move his body and what he can do with it. He can strive for higher levels of performance within his own limitations. Creativity in movement is limited only by each individual's physical and imaginative capabilities. Working on skills individually, he can discover many ways to use his head, neck, trunk, shoulders, arms, hands, legs, and feet. He can explore just how much he can use his afflicted legs (within the doctor's prescription). He can create and discover ways to throw a ball in more ways than a chest pass. Consequently, he gains more confidence in his ability to try other physical education activities such as games, self-testing activities, and rhythms. The handicapped child explores, discovers, and creates as many movements as possible.

Primary movements which can be attempted by the physically handicapped with varying degrees of success include:

Body awareness. Move head, neck, shoulders, arms, hands, trunk, legs, feet.

Spatial relationships. Have parts of the body in relation to objects in space; develop laterality and directionality.

Balance. Move in different directions and in various ways to develop dynamic and static balance; include activities requiring balancing of objects.

Axial movement. Raise the head while lying on the stomach; raise the arms and see what other parts of the body can be raised while lying on the stomach.

Swinging and swaying. Swing (sway) as many parts of the body as possible while sitting (lying); swing arm(s) in as many directions as possible while sitting; swing arms in circles (squares, triangles, rectangles, letter shapes, number formations).

Pushing and pulling. Push while sitting (lying down); show how many directions you can push something with hands (elbows, arms, trunk); pull while lying down; pull and/or push in an upward (downward, sideways) direction.

Bending and stretching. Bend different parts of the body while sitting (lying down); bend (stretch) parts of the body in as many directions as possible.

Twisting, turning, whirling. Show how many parts of the body can be twisted (turned, whirled) while sitting (lying down); twist the body in one direction (the other direction), to the right (left).

Shaking and beating. Show how many parts of the body can be shook while sitting (lying down, standing); shake the right (left) side of the body and beat with the left (right).

Locomotor movement. Walk with the class in a large circle without bumping anyone; walk toward a wall (object, person); do something else with the body while walking. While running, hopping, jumping, galloping, skipping, leaping, and sliding will generally be limited with cerebral palsied children, encourage them to develop their own patterns and movements for these activities—stimulate and challenge the creativity of the child.

There are many pieces of equipment which can be used in exploring movement. While it is difficult for Mickey to perform on balance beams, balance boards, hurdles, jump boards, saw horses, stairs, stilts, tables, and tires, he can be successful with others.

Balls. Throw the ball up and catch it (let it bounce before catching it); throw the ball in many different ways to a partner.

Bean bags. Do something with the bean bag; throw it up high and catch it; close your eyes and throw (toss) it from hand to hand.

Deck tennis rings. Throw the ring up in the air and catch it with two (one) hand(s); clap your hands once (twice, three, four) before catching it; catch the ring so it slides over an arm (both arms).

Hula hoops. Spin the hoop like an egg beater; throw the hoop in the air and catch it before it lands; whirl the hoop around an arm (both arms).

Wands. Balance on a wand; balance in different ways on the wand; drop the wand, let it bounce, and catch it in the air; balance the wand on the palm of a hand (on three, two, one finger(s)).

Ropes. Develop rope tricks involving upper trunk, arms, hands, and shoulders.

A very effective and challenging task for handicapped youngsters to solve can be simply stated, "What else can you do with your . . .?" In this way the individual has an opportunity to be creative and to build from his previous experiences. In particular, encourage these youngsters to think of and show movements and activities they have never seen performed previously.

Physically handicapped children do have a place in your physical education program just as much as Mickey has a place in my program. Classroom teachers and physical educators must be creative to survive in the world of children; *every* child, including the physically handicapped, has the potential to be creative.

Just as boys and girls in the special school for the handicapped created their own physical education activities, physically handicapped children in regular classrooms can create within their own sphere, in structured unit programs, and in movement exploration. Each child can be helped socially, emotionally, psychologically, and physically. No longer is it excusable—much less justifiable—for a little girl to sit on the sidelines and say wistfully, "I wish I could take physical education."

Suggested Resource Materials

And So They Move. 16mm, b&w, 19 min., sound. Available from Audio-Visual Center, Michigan State University, East Lansing, Michigan 48824. Deals with the application of movement to the physically handicapped. Children are encouraged to extend themselves in purposeful and enjoyable movement. Much of the program is built around improvised equipment—boxes, hoops, ropes, and benches—innovative indoor obstacle courses, and creative use of conventional playground equipment.

Physical Activities for the Mentally Retarded: Ideas for Instruction. AAHPER. Washington, D.C. 20036: NEA Publications-Sales, 1201 16th St., N.W., 1968. 137 pp. $2.00 Stock No. 245-07952. Includes activities, methods, and approaches readily adaptable for use in programs for the physically handicapped. Focus is on instruction in activities promoting fundamental motor development and the exploration of general areas of skill.

Physical Education: A Substitute for Hyperactivity and Violence
THOMAS EDSON

We owe it to emotionally and neurologically handicapped children to see what we can do in physical education to give them a sense of success. Physical education can help them gain peer status, a sense of belonging, and recognition, especially when they cannot gain it in academic pursuits. Children who are having difficulties in verbal pursuits often achieve success in nonverbal areas such as physical education. This gives them a "cushion" to fall back on for peer recognition and individual status while doing something challenging.

Immediate reinforcement from an arm around the shoulders or a pat on the back is just as meaningful as verbal approval. Recognition through presentations of ribbons, certificates, and similar awards may stimulate additional participation.

Children with emotional problems appear to perceive better through tactile and kinesthetic senses. For instance, they perceive better by moving their hands and arms through throwing and catching motions than by listening to directions only. A child's facial expressions and body gestures may suggest future actions; the instructor's ability to read this nonverbal communication may help him anticipate what will occur next.

Physical education helps children conform and establish routines which are especially beneficial for those who do not have established routines in their homes. Control of emotional patterns through physical activity is one of many ways to help children increase attention span, share, and await turns. Physical education can help children learn to sublimate personal desires for the sake of the group. Many emotionally handicapped children will relax under routine and orderly procedures; they feel secure in knowing what is coming next.

Physical education provides opportunities for children to conform to definite limits while providing tension-releasing outlets. Many activities and methods have been used with hyperactive children to give them purposeful movement in the classroom. Many hyperactive children feel more secure when surrounded with a great deal of equipment. They seem to remember better what they see than what they hear—demonstration and involvement are better than simply giving directions.

By providing various stations in the classroom such as listening posts, exercise stations—three-sided booths containing weights, stretchers, and similar devices—and other stations which provide opportunities for the child to release energy in a short period of time, a student can have a definite goal when he leaves his seat. Another station could contain mats where the child can perform exercises for release of tension, yet, where he has to contain himself within the definite limits of the mat. Gradually decrease the area of movement and increase the amount of time on the mat. Mats can also be used for relaxation exercises such as lying on the back with knees bent.

Written ball, jump rope, or balance beam progressions provide students with opportunities to carry out activities in a well-organized, sequential manner. Another technique which has proved very successful is to equip each child's desk with such equipment as hand grips, sponges, or other types of rubber devices to squeeze to release tension rather than allowing aggression to build; desk isometrics are also effective.

An effective approach on the playground is to spread out hula hoops with each containing tension-releasing devices as poi-poi balls, jump ropes, etc. Children stand inside the hoops and on a given command exchange stations. Start with a variety of stations so each child is active; rotate stations with a designated signal (whistle is blown, color called, number given). Gradually increase the activity time at each station.

Swimming and aquatic activities are important adjuncts to the total program. Water temperatures between 86 and 92 degrees seem to have calming effects upon hyperactive and emotionally disturbed children. Low-organized games such as "Squirrels in Trees" and "Musical Chairs" teach the child to withhold action until a whistle is blown or another stimulus is given.

Games such as "What Time Is It, Mr. Fox?" have definite lines and boundaries in which movements are controlled; these games also help children improve listening and concentration habits. Games like "Center-Catch Ball" can be used to teach awareness and alertness; most games involving use of balls help train easily distracted and hyperactive children in ocular pursuit activities. Likewise, dart and target games such as "Ring Toss," "Horseshoes," and "Dropping Clothespins in the Bottle" involve ocular pursuit.

Exercises such as swinging the arms loosely with head stationary and eyes straight ahead help the child to keep his body aligned and his eyes fixed. Many games and physical education activities provide awareness of lower and upper extremities and improve spatial relationships relative to exterior objects. Games can also provide rest and relaxation in which two or more children move while the rest stand or sit in a limited area.

Apparatus activities which follow definite progressions and sequences are excellent for motivation and can be used as task-reward reinforcement. Parachute progressions give release of energy in short periods of time. Balance beams and balance boards provide opportunities for better motor control in a limited area. Parallel bars, rings, and similar apparatus are motivational to the child and help focus attention to specific tasks. This is a form of reality therapy—he learns that if he doesn't concentrate he may fall off the apparatus.

Many times children with emotional problems become very hyperactive when they cannot meet the "stress of daily living." They withdraw and possibly develop indifferent attitudes; they feel they can protect themselves from failure and frustration by appearing indifferent. An important goal of physical education should be to develop and promote ways to communicate and help emotionally and neurologically handicapped children.

General Objectives of
Low Organized Games

1. Provide opportunities for success through simple progressions which become increasingly complex.
2. Provide opportunities for happiness, enjoyment, and fun.
3. Promote awareness of upper and lower extremities and of other parts of the body.
4. Develop laterality, directionality, and the ability to relate the body to external objects.
5. Increase attention span and concentration.
6. Build up visual, auditory, tactile, and kinesthetic memory.
7. Pace oneself according to the activity, i.e., adjust one's speed to the demands of the activity or game.
8. Help eliminate fear of motion.
9. Promote flexibility and ability to change.
10. Stimulate social interaction with peers and adults.
11. Teach control of movement patterns within definite set limits.
12. Stimulate use of all sensory mechanisms.
13. Increase coordination, agility, balance, endurance, power, speed, and similar motor and physical characteristics.

14. Release energy in short periods of time to reduce tensions.
15. Provide opportunities for recognition, success, good peer relations, belongingness, and status.
16. Promote overall body rhythm.

**Specific Objectives of Low
Organized Games**
What Time Is It, Mr. Fox?
1. Stay within set boundaries.
2. Improve listening habits and concentration.
3. Stress control of beginning and stopping an activity.
4. Restrict motor response until the appropriate stimulus is called.

Center-Catch Ball
1. Teach the names of classmates—this is especially good at the beginning of the school year or when a new student enters class.
2. Promote rest and relaxation when two children are active and the rest remain on the circle.
3. Promote awareness and alertness.
4. Control the ball within a limited area, i.e., the circle formed by players.

Squirrels in Trees
1. Promote spatial relations within a limited area.
2. Promote the ability to regain balance quickly after being in a confined space.
3. Develop lateral movement and peripheral vision.
4. Develop laterality and/or directionality.
5. Promote the ability to start and stop within a limited area.
6. Develop the ability to respond to a specific stimulus.

A Diversified Physical
Education Program
DONALD BILYEW

One of the major reasons that standard and generally accepted physical fitness programs have been found inadequate for meeting the unique needs of the handicapped child is because of the inability of these programs to adjust to the numerous and extensive individual differences found in groups of emotionally disturbed and mentally retarded children. Our aim is to provide a diversified program of developmental activities, games, sports, and rhythms suited to the interests, capacities, and limitations of each student. Creative movement or modern dance offers educational values not found in other types of physical education. Beyond the obvious values of dynamic movement and the development of agility, balance, coordination, endurance, and flexibility, lies the creative, expressive nature of dance.

As an art, dance offers an emotional outlet through spontaneous movements. When a child learns to control his body and finds the wide range of movement of which his body is capable, the sense of "self" becomes strengthened. Movement takes on new meaning. It becomes expressive. He has learned a new way to communicate.

The language of dance need not limit itself to any particular age group. With an imaginative approach, dance may become integrated in any school program. As a therapeutic agent, modern dance has successfully demonstrated its value to the total educational/recreation program.

Warm-ups are basic and form the basis of many dance movements. Through careful selection and with an active imagination, they are an easy natural transition to creativity in movement, which will become exaggerated and perhaps individualized or stylized.

Our girls have been exposed to modern dance for many years and have become increasingly receptive to going off campus to watch various dance performances. This year Devereux has contracted a professional dance teacher who comes into many of our units and works directly with the girls in creative movement.

Jogging

In the general area of recreation one encounters a great variety of physical types, from the fit and able, to those who are very limited. In providing an activity for all types of children, one often encounters great difficulty in involving those with severe limitations. Through the use of jogging it has been possible to evolve a program which allows children to participate in activities suited to their limitations as well as their needs.

Jogging is a fairly simple task. Defined, it is a progression of alternate walking and easy-paced running, i.e., trotting. When a program of jogging is followed, one can expect a strengthening of the muscles involved in running, of the heart, lungs, and the entire circulatory system. No special equipment or facilities are needed. This activity gives our limited children personal satisfaction and achievement in the area of physical education.

If a child performs at a marginal or better than marginal level, he is encouraged but not badgered for perfection of technique. As an aid to interest, a "Joggers' Record" is kept which shows the cumulative distance traveled. This record is displayed conspicuously for recognition of the students involved.

The acceptance of this program was beyond what we had hoped. Although frustration reactions and complaining were evidenced, they were handled with tact and understanding, always aiming for continued involvement. Even with our limited children, a wide variation in ability and strength was noted.

This shows the need for homogenous grouping of persons taking part in a jogging program. Generally, the use of a Joggers' Club is successful in giving our limited children exercise and involvement in a more effective manner.

Our specific program of jogging is based on the following principles:

1. The jogger works at a moderate rate of exertion.
2. A relatively high rate of exertion, i.e., trotting is followed by a period of mild exertion, i.e., walking.
3. There is a gradual increase in the length of the area for running and walking, and also in the number of run-walk cycles gone through per exercise period.
4. To sustain interest, a wide variety of routes are employed, some harder than others, with the ruggedness of the trail dictating the strenuousness of the program.

Obstacle Course

The obstacle course has a number of unique qualities: It is flexible, it does not exclude a person with limited physical abilities, and the course can provide choices. The individual is instructed to attempt only those obstacles that parallel his abilities. The entire course is self-testing.

Children who are fearful of failure in competitive situations enjoy the obstacle course because they cannot fail. As the child's confidence grows, he will attempt the more difficult areas. The obstacle course is competitive, which adds interest. By using time as a factor, intra-group, as well as competition with oneself is encouraged.

Circuit Course

At the Buttonwood Farms Camp, it has been found that a procedure which develops physical fitness and which best adjusts for individual differences is the circuit course. This combines the idea of an obstacle course with the concept of using different stations to develop various areas of the body. A child is expected to run from one station to another and perform various tasks or duties at, or while maneuvering through, each station or obstacle. Each step of this course is designed to elicit specific patterns of movement and behavior from the handicapped child.

The circuit course is not only easily adaptable for individual variations, but has proven effective in terms of eliciting the movements desired to develop specific physical skills. It has the added advantage of being a meaningful experience to the children from motivational and social standpoints, for activities are closely allied to the daily performances of the child. Also, it has the advantage of not requiring extensive explanations or training.

The following are typical activities used in this program: jogging, walking the balance beam, forward rolls across a mat, running backward, low obstacle jump, sprinting, zigzag running through a positioned group of medicine balls, hopping to the next station, crab walk under a series of obstacles, telephone climb, tunnel crawl, uphill sprint, deep breathing and shoulder shrugs.

The equipment used includes safety cones, climbing ropes, balance beams, parallel bars, Swedish box, balls, and mats. In due time there is considerable improvement in the children's agility, coordination, endurance, athletic skills, and strength.

WHAT DID THEY LEARN

Introduction To Section III

Testing is a term used to refer to the evaluation of status. An increase in an individual's status indicates an improvement in performance which is frequently closely related to learning. Teachers can test their students periodically to determine if improvement is taking place.

Although directed at the student, intelligent testing can reveal much about a physical education program and the teaching techniques involved. The articles in this section were selected so that the reader could gain an understanding of both testing in the elementary school and program evaluation.

CHAPTER VI

THE VALUE OF TESTING

Evaluation in the Elementary Physical Education Program
STRATTON F. CALDWELL

Evaluation is an ongoing process of continual appraisal and assessment of change, dependent upon value judgements determined by selective criteria. The process of evaluation is concerned with where we were, where we are now, what and how well we are doing, and where we are going. This process is in action constantly, as all of us must discriminate, choose and make decisions relative to our objectives, goals, purposes and aims. We are constantly weighing what we see and understand in relation to goals and purposes, and the progress or movement towards them.

Facets of Evaluation

Evaluation is concerned with all facets of learning, and involves the teacher and all pupils. As teachers we are vitally interested in children's past experiences and current achievement as it affects next steps toward goals. We are deeply concerned with the interests, drives, abilities, beliefs, personality, behavior and physical well being of children. We examine changes in growth and development of the total organism as it moves toward fulfillment of aims, objectives, goals. We are always involved with status quo as it helps reach desired outcomes, recognizing however, that appraisal of status quo may sway our judgement of achievement if not carefully analyzed. An uncritical overemphasis upon norms may result in pronouncements signifying finality or permanence. Let us see normative judgements as but one step in the right direction toward fulfillment of desired ends. In the final analysis, the value of education or learning is demonstrated by change in individual response or behavior. Evaluation, thus, is the examination of this change in light of established, accepted goals.

Textbook Interpretation of Evaluation

Textbooks concerned with physical education experiences designed for the elementary school child vary enormously in depth and breadth of interpretation and understanding of the role of the evaluative process at this level. An examination of over twenty-five texts revealed that evaluation does not appear to assume a role of major importance to many authors at this level. Almost 25 percent of this resource material made no provision for evaluation or presented a most limited interpretation of the concept. The texts which included the evaluation concept almost always made provision in terms of a separate section or entire chapter.

Many authors introduced the concept of evaluation in its broadest interpretation and then delimited evaluation and measuring instruments into qualitative and quantitative context. The more prevalent terminology included the words *subjective* and *objective* as methods or techniques of aiding in the identification of outcomes.

The Whole Child

Somewhat alarming is the realization that even in many of our current physical education textbooks focused on children of elementary school age, the child is still split up into the motor self, emotional self, social self and intellectual self without returning the parts to form the *whole* organism again. Perhaps the most common offense is the disproportionate amount of space devoted to analysis and evaluation of motor skills with little or no relationship to the whole child and "why" it is important for the child to possess such skills. Even in growth and development texts the organism usually starts out as a whole, but is quickly differentiated into the physical, social, emotional and intellectual, and is indeed difficult to recognize again as a complete reassembled totality.

If evaluation could always be related to the child, rather than to a specific movement skill, pattern or experience per se, it would be ongoing rather than an end in itself. If we believe that each child is a unique individual and develops according to a pattern peculiar to his own growth rate, it is indeed difficult to justify a disproportionate use of norms and averages when attempting to measure individual achievement of children. If authors would clarify the concept that a norm or achievement scale is merely an indicator, a means to an end, perhaps such evaluation devices would not be regarded as the ultimate answer or criterion of finality.

Concluding Statement

A concept that needs clarification and greater emphasis today in physical education texts dealing with the elementary age child is the recognition of the role of the child in the evaluative process. The child is not a passive organism that will adapt and adjust flexibly to all adult determined goals and objectives. The child will learn as he becomes part of the total process of determining goals, and as he relates them to his interests, desires and needs. The child must be taken from where he is at a given time in the educational process and provided experiences that will stimulate him to progress toward maturity at his own developmental rate.

A Gap in the Elementary School
Testing Program
T. M. Scott

Recently I heard a panel discussion at a P-T-A meeting. Four people—a clinical psychologist, an elementary school principal, and two persons from the county testing program, discussed current testing procedures. Mimeographed material was passed out showing which tests are used, at what age and grade, and the discussion centered around the selection and use of these tests at various elementary and junior high school grade levels. It was generally agreed that testing the intellectual, academic, social, emotional, and vocational aspects of the individual is valuable. But I was shocked to realize that no consideration had been given to testing the physical or physiological potential of the child at these grade levels.

We accept the fact that it is worthwhile to know what we can expect the child to learn, and at what rate; what academic skills he has already achieved; what his vocational aptitudes and interests are; and in some cases what his social competence and emotional stability may be, compared to others his age. Yet how can these areas of potential and achievement, so clearly interrelated insofar as the functional capacity of the individual is concerned, be clearly divided, and the physical or physiological aspects be ignored?

Looking back at our progress in measuring potential and evaluating achievement, it seems strange that the area of "organic vigor," which is one of the cardinal objectives of education, has been so neglected by the very people who claim to be interested in "the whole child." Perhaps the testing authorities are unaware that measures do exist by which we could assess the physical aspects of the child. Perhaps the leaders of elementary school physical education have hesitated too long in seeking the initiative to show the value of diagnostic and achievement tests. Use of these tests would give valuable information concerning the child at a stage of development when some worthwhile steps could be taken to improve the physical aspects of his total growth pattern.

Children are driven to the front door of the school and picked up there at the end of the school day. They sit motionless in front of television sets. Some of the space which used to be available for vigorous play is now occupied by temporary classroom buildings. Even riding a bicycle has become an increasingly hazardous activity, with more and higher powered automobiles on every road and street. Additionally, we are now becoming a nation of overweight people, eating more and moving about less, thus laying the groundwork early for the nation's number one killer, heart disease.

In some cases children are already being tested in an attempt to find out simply whether they are weak or strong. But these cases are few, being left solely to an interested person or as an indirect outcome of a physical examination. Even in these few cases, this information is not integrated with other facts which lead to guiding and counseling pupils in areas of their weaknesses. If it may be assumed that the total growth potential of the child is important, and that we should know as much as we possibly can about him, then it must become the responsibility of the school to include testing the physical or physiological potential of the child and making it a part of his total growth record.

At present, in most elementary schools, and in some junior high schools, the physical activities are planned and supervised by classroom teachers, and not by trained physical educators. This should not preclude the possibility of administering simple batteries of tests by people already trained in testing, who are responsible for planning and administering the overall testing program. These people use the test results for general guidance purposes only. They are not necessarily familiar with the specialized procedures which may be used to correct deficiencies or deviations found as a result of the tests which they administer. This is done, in fact, by people trained in specialized areas; the teacher of the accelerated classroom, the remedial reading teacher, the clinical psychologist, the retarded group teacher, and the vocational guidance resource person.

It is as important to determine which child is physically weak, and may need help in maintaining sufficient strength to carry him through the school day, as it is to measure the other qualities. The trend now seems to be to turn out as many nuclear physicists and biochemists as possible, in the shortest time possible. But to what advantage, if they do not have enough organic vigor to carry them through the work day? With the added burdens of achievement which we have placed on the child, it appears that some instrument of motivation should be used to make him and his parents aware of possible weaknesses in his physical make-up. Research and investigation has shown that if man does not use his body in dynamic activity and movement, he may regress from a robust, highly functional organism to an inefficient, poorly functioning one.

If physical activity is construed to be a worthwhile educational endeavor, then physical tests and test results should also be evaluated to give a picture of the child as a total individual.

Physical Fitness Appraisal in the Primary Grades

WILLIAM F. STRAUB AND A. MAE TIMER

Physical fitness is an important objective of physical education at all grade levels—kindergarten through college. Currently, physical fitness appraisal and guidance does not usually begin until grade four. This policy seems to be inconsistent with sound educational philosophy which suggests that evaluation should be an integral part of the teaching-learning process. Clarke (1) lends credence to the above thought when he said: "A truly great society must rest basically upon physically fit children and adults. Continuance of a generally low level of physical fitness is a shocking waste of human resources."

First Physical Education Teachers

If physical education is an attitude and a way of life—for a life time, we must begin the educative process at a very early age. Steinhaus (6), sensing the importance of physical education at an early age, said: "Mothers are our first physical education teachers."

Psychological and sociological studies on the development of attitudes and learning indicate that meaningful experiences should begin at a very early age. Head Start and all other pre-kindergarten programs are based upon the above premise. This is the time that we must help children to explore the *what, how, when, who, where, and why* of physical education. This is the time when the values of total fitness, including physical fitness, should be initiated.

Physically Active Parents

It is not surprising to find that research supports the hypothesis that: Physically active parents tend to have physically active children. Ruffer's study (4) presents evidence that high school pupils who are physically active are given significantly better examples to follow concerning physical activity than are inactive students. Fathers of physically active students are physically more active and give their children more encouragement to participate in vigorous activities than is true of inactive students. Thus, the need for inculcating desirable habits, attitudes, and knowledges toward physical activity at an early age is clearly established.

Fitness Poorest At The Elementary School Level

A 1965 New York State physical fitness survey (5) involving 130,044 boys and girls, grades 4-12, shows that physical fitness is poorest at the elementary school levels and improves from the junior high to the senior high school level. Factors that may be responsible for this finding are: the gradual disappearance of recess periods, increased academic demands on elementary school pupils, television, and infrequent physical education periods in the primary grades. Even though the daily physical education period is becoming a trend, it has not been implemented in many schools.

Appraisal Begins At Grade Four

Except in a few isolated instances, physical fitness appraisal usually begins at grade four. As a result, physically underdeveloped primary grade pupils are not identified and therefore, do not receive any assistance with special developmental activities which would help them improve their physical fitness. The need for the development of a valid, reliable, and objective primary grade physical fitness test is clearly evident.

The Measuring Instrument

The measuring instrument must be suitable for the particular age, growth, and maturational characteristics of primary grade pupils. The test items must be fun for the pupils to perform so that they will willingly practice them during out-of-class hours. Good use must be made of test results. Testing for testing sake is committing educational treason.

Except for the work of Hanson[2] and Kirchner[3], very little has been done in the area of primary grade physical fitness test development. Until greater attention is focused upon this topic, primary grade children will continue to be subjected to unscientific activity regimens.

Suggestions To Help Teachers

Despite a dearth of scientifically designed tests to accurately measure the physical fitness status of primary grade children, *an imaginative teacher can do much to help children* improve their physical fitness. It is absolutely important that children, at an early age, learn to enjoy physical activity. If they learn to love to play vigorous games and contests, increments in balance, speed, endurance, and other fitness components will be forthcoming.

The game or *"fun approach"* to physical activity is the type of pedagogy which every teacher should explore. Even the obese child, caught in the spirit of the games, can find that extending his muscles can be fun.

The teacher, of course, *sets the tempo* and controls the educational climate of the class. If the teacher loves children and enjoys seeing them participate in physical activity, much can be accomplished.

Generally, the most successful elementary physical education teachers have found that *teacher participation in the games* helps to foster excellent pupil-teacher relationships. "The teach by example approach," has always been one of our most successful teaching methods. Teachers have found that even those children who are not particularly adept in the classroom will try harder if the teacher has gained their confidence on the playing field or in the gymnasium.

Experienced teachers are able to appraise the physical fitness status of their pupils by watching them participate in organized and free-play activities. The boy or girl who cannot travel across the horizontal ladder or climb a rope is lacking in upper arm and/or girdle strength. The youngster who cannot jump rope, walk the balance beam or perform similar physical skills is obviously not physically fit.

Use Information

Teachers who are aware of the physical developmental process put this information to use. They carefully modify the activity regimen of their pupils so that greater attention is directed toward those activities which are needed. Perhaps pogo sticks are utilized by those boys and girls who need to develop better balance, wheelbarrow races are employed to help those pupils who need to improve upper arm and shoulder girdle strength and other activities are specifically designed to meet physical needs; and most important,

Johnny doesn't even realize that he is getting the treatment. The "fun approach" is still very much in vogue.

SELECTED BIBLIOGRAPHY

1. Clarke, H. Harrison. "Physical Fitness Newsletter #1"; September, 1966; University of Oregon; Eugene, Ore.
2. Hanson, Margie R. "Motor Performance Testing of Elementary School Age Children," Unpublished Doctoral Dissertation, University of Washington, Seattle, Washington, 1965, p. 270.
3. Kirchner, Glenn. *Physical Education for Elementary School Children.* Wm. C. Brown Company, Dubuque, Iowa, 1966, p. 655.
4. Ruffer, W. A. "A Study of Extreme Physical Activity Groups of Young Men." Research Quarterly, 36: May, 1965, p. 183.
5. Straub, William F. "New York State Physical Fitness Survey." New York State Education Department, Albany, New York, 1965.
6. Steinhaus, A. H. "Toward An Understanding of Health and Physical Education." Dubuque, Iowa, Wm. C. Brown Company, 1963. p. 28.

Sizing Up
Your School's Phys Ed

Can your 12-year-old son chin himself, do 14 consecutive sit-ups and, in a ten-second period, complete four squat thrusts? Can your teen-age daughter do three squat thrusts in ten seconds, eight modified pull-ups and ten sit-ups? Do they even know what these simple exercises are? If the answers are no, it may be because your school system is shortchanging them in an important area of their education–physical fitness.

Physical fitness, when used by professionals in the physical education field, refers not to the building of a star athlete, but to developing the ability of every student to use and properly care for his body. To neglect it, they argue, invites physical and emotional problems that may plague him as an adult.

There's convincing evidence of the soundness of this theory. Physical inactivity and obesity are among the factors identified by the American Heart Association as linked with a high risk of heart attack. Psychologists stress the need for adolescents to feel that they belong, that they are part of the in group, a feeling that team sports can help provide. And educators find that youngsters who participate in vigorous physical activity tend to be more alert, better-rounded students.

Every Day ... or Hardly Ever?

Ideally, to meet students' needs, physical education would be required on a daily basis from kindergarten through high school; the minimum recommendation is three times a week over the same period. But 14% of the nation's schoolchildren do not participate in any physical education program at all; and another 27% are in programs rated less than adequate. Only California and Massachusetts require daily physical education classes for all grades, and the Massachusetts law, passed in 1966, is not yet fully implemented. Although most other states have some physical education requirements, the standards all too often are vague; enforcement of them is lax; and implementation, left to the individual schools, ranges from excellent to nonexistent.

The problem is compounded by a shortage of well-trained health and physical education instructors, particularly women teachers. Many schools lack the facilities to carry on an adequate program, even if well-trained instructors were available. As a result, what purports to be school-wide physical education may be no more than a proving ground for varsity team players, while less-talented, less-developed students spend their class time standing around watching or making scrapbooks of various sports events.

The picture isn't all dark, though. For the past several decades, the American Association of Health, Physical Education and Recreation, a department of the National Education Association, has vigorously promoted improved health and physical education standards in state school systems. Since 1961, the President's Council on Physical Fitness has conducted a nation-wide campaign to make the public aware of the need to improve the physical fitness of the population as a whole. As a result of their combined efforts, 32 states have improved standards in the past seven years, either by law or regulation.

Using a test for evaluating physical fitness, AAHPER has conducted two nationwide surveys of students aged 10 through 17 in 2,500 schools. A comparison of test results shows marked improvement among the students, an indication that schools are expanding and upgrading their programs.

The President's Council and AAHPER jointly developed the Presidential Physical Fitness Award program to recognize students who score in the top 16% on all seven items of the AAHPER test. Last year, more than 50,000 boys and girls qualified for the award.

In cooperation with the council, many states have established Demonstration Centers, schools that can be visited by parents or educators interested in seeing a good program in operation. Your state department of education can tell you whether there's one near you.

Exercise for Everyone

Adequate facilities and a trained staff are key elements in an outstanding program. For example, Wood Junior High School in

Rockville, Md., employs six full-time physical education instructors for a student body of 1,000 sixth, seventh and eighth graders. Facilities include a regulation-size gymnasium, smaller separate boys' and girls' gyms and outdoor playing fields. In another year tennis courts will be added.

Each child has a full hour of physical education every day. The emphasis at Wood is on promoting sound physical condition and growth. Students work their way through the gamut of activities. In addition, the program for boys includes soccer, touch football, basketball, cross country, gymnastics, wrestling, track and field competition, softball, archery, badminton, table tennis, volleyball and even dancing. The girls' program is pretty much the same, omitting football, cross country and wrestling and placing more emphasis on gymnastics and modern dance.

The school supplements its regular physical education courses with intramural sports, which begin at the end of the school day and attract 75% of the students. It's a department rule that any student who signs up to play in an intramural contest *must* play, so that no child, no matter how inept he may be, is left standing on the sidelines. The school participates to a small extent in extramural sports, informal contests with other schools, and the same rule applies there. All children are eligible to compete in any extramural sport.

Wood also provides a modified program on a daily basis for children who are unable to take the regular course or who need special attention. This group includes those with low motor coordination, those who are underdeveloped or obese and those who may have some limiting physical condition, such as a heart disease. Each child is evaluated individually and his activity is designed to work around his defect and still allow him to develop to the fullest extent of his ability. A set of goals is drawn up, to be reached by Thanksgiving, February, Easter and the close of school. The system, in addition to promoting a competitive spirit, allows students to see their accomplishments. Some of them improve enough to go into the regular program.

A bonus from all this attention to physical development is that it generates a tremendous amount of school spirit—among both students and their parents—which carries over into all the other school activities.

Programs such as the one offered at Wood are on the increase, particularly in junior high schools and, to some extent, in elementary schools. But when students reach the high school level, physical education often is required for only one or two years. Even then, the school can do much to encourage continuing physical development.

At Washington-Lee High School in Arlington, Va., physical education is required only in the 10th and 11th grades. But a number of years ago the school inaugurated an intramural program to supplement the regular physical education courses and to encourage students to continue physical development. The program is given precedence over interscholastic sports; for example, varsity teams must take second place in scheduling the use of facilities and equipment. Intramural sports attract about half of Washington-Lee's 2,000 students. Girls in the program participate in extramural sports only to the extent of scheduling "play days" with other schools in the area; boys have a variety of varsity and junior varsity teams to move up to. Varsity and junior varsity athletes can take part in the intramural program, but are ineligible to play in any sport in which they are interscholastic team members.

What to Ask Your School

Not all schools, of course, have the staff or the facilities to schedule programs such as the ones described here. But with the backing of parents and school administrators, every school can have some kind of program. The President's Council recommends that every child be given opportunity for sustained vigorous exercise every day, which can be accomplished even without a trained staff or elaborate equipment.

For a more comprehensive program, the recommendation for grades one through six is one period per day, five days a week, minimum of 30 minutes, exclusive of recess and time spent in dressing and showering; for grades seven through twelve, one standard class period a day, five days a week. The program should apply to all students, permitting no substitution of band, ROTC, athletic programs or other extracurricular activities for regular physical education class work. It should include intramural and extramural sports for all boys and girls in grades four through twelve, with interscholastic sports programs available for athletically gifted youngsters. Qualified teachers should be employed to conduct these activities.

Using those recommendations as a guideline, ask yourself the following questions about your child's physical education program.

How many times a week does he have physical education?

How much time a day is devoted to actual physical activity, either exercises or participation in some sport?

If the school program includes team sports, does he *always* get a turn during his class period?

Is there an intramural program, and does signing up for it assure him of active participation?

Is there an extramural program, and is it open to all students? Is he regularly tested for physical ability and improvement?

With all the emphasis on academic achievement, physical education may not seem so important to you now. But to compete in a world growing ever more complex, not only your child's mind but his body must be trained to stand the pace. The place to begin is in school, so that by the time he is an adult, fitness will have become a habit.